Cyberdualism in China

Internet usage in China has recently grown exponentially, rising from 59 million users in 2002 to 710 million by mid-2016. One in every two Chinese has
currently been exposed to the Internet. This upsurge has made political communication among citizens and between the government and citizens less
costly and almost instantaneous in China. Despite these advances, scholars
are only beginning to understand and systematically explain the ways in
which increased Internet exposure may affect behavior and values of Chinese netizens. Can the Internet help liberalize Chinese society due to its
innate pluralism? Has the Internet become an efficient tool assisting the ruling elite to remain in power, given the tendency of Internet service providers
and users to be easily manipulated by the Chinese state?

   This book addresses these questions by focusing on the most digitally
embedded segment of Chinese population – university students. Using
survey evidence from more than 1200 observations, data confirm that
Internet exposure to information generated by fellow netizens promotes
democratic orientation, enhances political resistance to indoctrination, and
boosts popular nationalism. However, exposure to government-managed
websites encourages regime support and, at a less significant level, decreases
democratic orientation and elevates official patriotism. People who perceive
the Internet as a tool enhancing the vertical communication between the
Chinese government and netizens tend to be patriotic and supportive of the
regime. Building upon quantitative evidence, this book draws a nuanced
picture of Internet exposure and its political implications.

Shiru Wang is Research Associate at Hong Kong Institute of Asia-Pacific
Studies, The Chinese University of Hong Kong.

Routledge Contemporary China Series

Cyberdualism in China

The Political Implications of Internet
Exposure of Educated Youth

Shiru Wang

Routledge
Taylor & Francis Group

LONDON AND NEW YORK

First published 2017
by Routledge

2 Park Square, Milton Park, Abingdon, Oxfordshire OX14 4RN
52 Vanderbilt Avenue, New York, NY 10017

Routledge is an imprint of the Taylor & Francis Group, an informa business

First issued in paperback 2018

British Library Cataloguing-in-Publication Data
A catalogue record for this book is available from the British Library

Library of Congress Cataloging-in-Publication Data
A catalog record for this book has been requested

ISBN: 978-1-138-21804-8 (hbk)
ISBN: 978-0-367-14185-1 (pbk)

Typeset in Times New Roman
by Apex CoVantage, LLC

This book is dedicated to my son, who is the most beautiful thing that has ever happened to me and who redefines me.

Contents

List of figures

List of tables

Acknowledgments

Upon graduating with my PhD, I worked at the University of Hong Kong (HKU) as a postdoctoral fellow. My supervisor, Prof. Gerard Postiglione, generously granted me great autonomy that most postdoctoral fellows in Hong Kong academic institutions were not entitled to. I became interested in the Internet usage of university students, the future elite of China. The Internet penetration in China started to gain momentum around the mid-2000s and increased rapidly afterward, especially among educated young elite. Sharing the same curiosity with many others, I wondered whether this increasingly salient development exhibits any systematic effect on individual Chinese and the political system.

With an HKU research grant, I conducted a survey among university students, from which data used in this book originated. To solely manage a large-scale survey was an amazing experience for a fresh graduate who had only conducted research with a team. I had figured that this project would be a rather lonely journey, but thanks to a number of colleagues and friends, as well as my family, I did not feel that way.

On top of my thank-you list is Prof. Postiglione. As a supportive and generous mentor, Prof. Postiglione helped me in every possible way, not only with this project, but also with other matters. I deeply appreciate the warm welcome and heartfelt encouragement he has given me. Along with his wife, Prof. Zhang Li-fang, they immediately eased my anxiety as a newcomer to Hong Kong and HKU.

Another great life mentor of mine, Prof. Deborah Davis, who I have known for more than a decade, read and commented on an excerpt of this book. As always, her insights enlightened me.

I extend my gratitude to my friends and colleagues, Prof. Pierre Landry, Prof. Gong Ting, Dr. Kang Yi, Dr. Ling Minhua, and Mr. Jiang Niantao, and to the two anonymous reviewers of my book proposal. Their comments on either the entire project or specific issues were substantially helpful. I am grateful toward my two research assistants, as well as the survey teams, for their wonderful work. I also want to thank HKU and the City University of Hong Kong for their financial and other support during my research.

Finally, I want to thank my parents who gave up their leisure time and helped me take care of my newborn child so that I could concentrate on my writing. There would not be this book if not for them.

1   Understanding the Internet

Introduction

Internet usage in China has recently grown exponentially, rising from 59 million users in 2002 to 710 million by mid-2016 (China Internet Network Information Center [CNNIC], July 2016). One in every two Chinese has currently been exposed to the Internet. This upsurge has made political communication among citizens and between the government and citizens less costly and almost instantaneous. Despite these advances, scholars are only beginning to understand and systematically explain the ways in which increased Internet exposure may affect behavior and values of Chinese citizens. Can the Internet help liberalize Chinese society due to its innate pluralism? Has the Internet become an efficient tool assisting the ruling elite to remain in power, given the tendency of Internet service providers and users to be easily manipulated by the Chinese state?

Although these seemingly diverging effects have often been recognized and discussed in research, scholars disagree upon the implications. Western-centrism drives researchers to discern any sign of democracy, which is the presumed destination for authoritarian regimes, and quickly conclude that authoritarianism will be terminated, or at least greatly weakened, soon by the liberal trend. Ever since the 1990s when the Internet became widely involved in the lives of the Chinese, optimism rapidly spread in scholarly studies, which declared the Internet a platform to breed liberal views and asserted that the increasing liberalism originating from the Internet would strengthen civil society, promote political liberalization, and ultimately fuel democratization in China (Lagerkvist, 2010; Yang, 2005 and 2009; Tai, 2004 and 2006; Esarey and Xiao, 2011; Zheng, 2008; Tong and Lei, 2013; Zhou, 2009).

By contrast, another group of scholars emphasize that Internet freedom is merely a result of tolerance and acquiescence of the state, which is always capable of ending pluralism on the Internet at any moment through a series of strategies, from hard and direct censorship (e.g., shutdown and blocking) to newly invented soft and indirect strategies (MacKinnon, 2007 and 2011; Brady, 2008; Kalathil and Boas, 2003; Zheng, 2008). According to this group of scholars, the ultimate winner in this game via the Internet is likely the state, and Chinese netizens cannot incite a regime change through the Internet under current institutional settings.

Another group of scholars (Herold, 2011; Marolt, 2011) propose that this dichotomy between the state and netizens is not always relevant. If Internet users always ignore the surveillance and censorship imposed by the state and the latter "fades into the background and ceases to be a motivating or influencing factor for the individual Internet user," then the state's control over the Internet will not entail any behavioral correction among Internet users (Marolt, 2011, p. 58).

The Internet is an institution (Lagerkvist, 2010; Herold, 2011), and the different understandings of the Internet lead to various conclusions about its political effects, which are captured by the following metaphors.

Panopticism of the Internet

The concept of the panopticon is borrowed to describe the intensive surveillance and censorship imposed on the Internet within China (Marolt, 2011). The panopticon, originally designed by Jeremy Bentham, is a disciplinary institutional system that upholds a power relationship by imposing an Orwellian supervision over people. It is structured as follows:

> at the periphery, annular building; at the centre, a tower; this tower is pierced with wide windows that open onto the inner side of the ring; the peripheric building is divided into cells, each of which extends the whole width of the building; they have two windows, one on the inside, corresponding to the windows of the tower; the other, on the outside, allows the light to cross the cell from one end to the other. All that is needed, then, is to place a supervisor in a central tower and to shut up in each cell a madman, a patient, and a condemned man, a worker or a schoolboy. By the effect of backlighting, one can observe from the tower, standing out precisely against the light, the small captive shadows in the cells of the periphery.
>
> (Foucault, 1977, p. 200)

The institution guarantees that "each individual is constantly located, examined and distributed" (Foucault, 1977, p. 197). "[T]he inmate must never know whether he is being looked at any one moment; but he must be sure that he may always be so" (Foucault, 1977, p. 201). Foucault (1977) argues that the panoptic surveillance tends to deter the defiance of inmates. The

Chinese Communist Party state employs multiple means to guarantee a tight control over the Internet and thus maintain the level of panopticism of the Internet.

Surveillance and censorship

In 2005, an estimate of more than 30,000 Internet police scrutinized the cyberspace and immediately erased posts believed to be harmful because they contained pornography, rumors, or criticism against the party state (Watts, 2005). Around mid-2006, the Shenzhen government decided to make Internet police visible to further deter potential offenses. Two cartoon mascots called "Jingjing" and "Chacha" appeared on all websites accessed in Shenzhen; the presence of these characters encouraged self-regulation and reminded Internet users that they were supervised (Dickie, 2006; Marolt, 2011). The online images of Internet police reinforce panopticism by promoting a sense of continuous surveillance. The line between acceptable and unacceptable content in cyberspace is deliberately left blurred, generating an uncertain atmosphere that causes citizens to remain cautious about what they say online (Marolt, 2011).

Censorship limits the access of Internet users to the outside World Wide Web (WWW) to maintain "the closing of the town" (Foucault, 1977, p. 195). The sovereignty of the state over the Internet within China is derived from the fact that the government literally owns bandwidth and that private companies have to rent it to provide Internet service. The state is capable of upholding the "Great Firewall of China" (GFC) through regulations and technical maneuvers (Fallows, 2008; Herold, 2011). The GFC results in the slow access and loading speed of websites outside China, discouraging casual viewing. Particular websites can be permanently or temporarily blocked from Chinese Internet users, causing "quasi-separation" between the Internet within China and the rest of the WWW (Herold, 2011). Blacklisting words deemed sensitive or offensive is another censorship strategy. When an Internet user within China attempts to view websites containing sensitive terms or phrases, Internet connection is intercepted. For instance, terms related to the Tiananmen Square Movement in 1989, Falun Gong, and the independence of Tibet are all blocked. The websites of human rights groups and Western and Taiwanese media are also frequently blocked (The Guardian, July 16, 2002). At different critical periods, the list of offensive terms is often modified, and users usually have to identify sensitive terms through trial and error.

Self-censorship

More importantly, Internet companies in China are urged by the state to impose a strong self-censorship. The public pledge of self-regulation and professional ethics for the Internet industry in China was launched by the Internet Society of China, a semigovernment organization, in 2002. After the launching, not only large web giants based in the country (e.g., Baidu, Sina, and Sohu) and universities (e.g., Peking and Qinghua Universities), but also foreign companies (e.g., Yahoo!) chose to sign and abide by the pledge because these entities depend on the state's approval to operate (The Guardian, July 16, 2002). According to the pledge, Internet companies should be "[r]efraining from producing, posting or disseminating pernicious information that may jeopardize state security and disrupt social stability . . . Monitor the information publicized by users on websites according to law and remove the harmful information promptly."[1] Some companies take proactive actions and engage in internal oversight by training self-discipline commissioners (Xiao, August 29, 2010).[2]

A reputation mechanism has also been adopted by the state to encourage the compliance of Internet companies. The Internet Society of China grants adhering Internet companies the China Internet Self-Discipline Award on a regular basis.[3] This award recognizes companies for creating "harmonious and healthy Internet development" (MacKinnon, 2011, p. 35). Since 2008, this government-affiliated organization has also worked as a credit rating agency that evaluates the performance of Internet companies and publicizes their ratings.[4] Large Internet companies, including Baidu, Tencent, Sina, and Sohu, managed to be rated the best.[5] Recent official news also indicated that the Chinese government planned to embed the Internet police in major Internet companies to impose further surveillance on both netizens and web enterprises (Dou, 2015).

Thus, the institutional organization of the Internet industry in China enables the state to impose panoptic surveillance by directly supervising individual users and penetrating into Internet service providers. Profit-seeking Internet companies in China often choose to cooperate with the state (Stockmann, 2013; Stockmann and Gallagher, 2011). The state remains capable of further intervening in online communication when necessary. Control is tighter than normal during certain periods. For instance, Internet users have been facing a series of tightenings under the current Xi-Li administration since 2013. A series of campaigns in 2013 strongly signaled ideological rectification. Influential bloggers (big Vs) were harassed, and some were arrested. The next round of government-led campaigns for web cleaning followed immediately in 2014, which combated online pornography, violence, and rumors (Rose and Roche, 2014). Since 2015, popular virtual private networks (VPNs) that grant Chinese Internet users encrypted channels to uncensored servers to "climb over the Great Firewall" and circumvent domestic censorship such as Astrill, have begun to be blocked (Chen et al., 2015; Griffiths, 2015). Has the Internet literally become the panopticon? The big data generated through the new media make surveillance more efficient than the pre-Internet age (McMullan, July 23, 2015). But, one feature of the panopticon that immediately invalidates the Internet is the division of inmates. Individuals are isolated in separated cells in the panopticon. By contrast, the Internet grants opportunities for netizens to network and even organize and mobilize a collective action. Therefore, rather than panopticism, some scholars emphasize the pluralistic nature of the Internet and propose that the Internet functions as a public sphere.

The Internet as the public sphere

The Internet, particularly Web 2.0 and above, is intrinsically different from older media instruments in that it flattens the structure of communication and transforms it from media centered to citizen centered. Rather than remaining a passive receiver of information, a netizen can initiate and contribute to communication with other netizens. The CNNIC (July 2016) data show that half of the Chinese population experiences convenient and inexpensive access to the Internet as a result of the technological advancement. Particularly with a rapid proliferation of smartphones, individuals are networked as long as their phones are connected to a telecommunications network. Netizens may outperform Internet police by reposting in a large group simultaneously, which may de facto delay and even bypass censorship. Although the state is very capable of delaying data transferring and slowing down the loading speed of some websites, the Internet has overall compressed time and space and enabled netizens to network and spread the word efficiently. The decentralizing nature of the Internet has weakened the surveillance and censorship imposed by the state. Thus, the innate pluralism of the Internet promotes efficient communication between netizens, and greatly reduces panopticism.

Habermas' (1989) concept of the public sphere is introduced to capture this nature of the Internet in scholarly studies. The Internet is believed to establish a public agenda and grant a place for public deliberation that is at least partially independent from the control of the state; therefore, the Internet has engendered a politically opinionated public who is either critical of the regime or supportive of democratic norms (Esarey and Xiao, 2008; Xiao, 2011; Lei, 2011; Sullivan, 2012; Tang and Huhe, 2014; Tang and Sampson, 2012; Tang and Yang, 2011; Tong and Lei, 2013; Yang, 2005, 2009; Zhou, 2009). This view is upheld by the fact that netizens systematically engage in whistleblowing and citizen journalism and even organize collective actions via the Internet.

Whistleblowing

Spontaneous anticorruption attempts have helped identify a number of corrupt local officials by online whistleblowing. Some corrupt officials were caught because their properties, which cost beyond their financial capacities, were exposed by netizens. Examples include Zhou Jiugeng and Zhai Zhenfeng, both of whom were local district government officials, and Gong Aiai, a local bank official. Corrupt officials were also caught because of records of promiscuous sexual behavior, which implied exchanges between sex and power that were leaked online. Examples are Mei Guosheng, Han Feng, Wu Zhiming, and Lei Zhengfu.

Another type of whistleblowing is not related to the personal lives of local officials. For instance, documents leaked online in April 2011 revealed that Sinopec, one of the state-owned petroleum giants in China, purchased expensive liquor that cost $245,000 using company money. This incident finally led to the dismissal of the Guangdong branch chief (Higgins, 2011).

Zhu Rifeng, a former migrant worker and a widely acknowledged citizen journalist, represents a group of whistleblowers online. He orchestrated the resignation of Lei Zhengfu by uploading his sexual videos on the Web, and he has established and run a website called People's Supervision Net to reveal suspicious cases of corruption since 2006. As of early 2013, he claimed that he had already exposed 100 officials, one-third of which were actually prosecuted (Jacobs, 2013).

Citizen journalism

Aside from whistleblowing, Chinese netizens can influence public affairs by acting as citizen journalists, closely watching the development of public events, proactively expressing their opinions, and even pursuing offline investigations. When Deng Yujiao, a waitress in a township hotel, stabbed some township officials who attempted to rape her in 2009, netizens even stepped out of the cyberspace, helped Deng and her parents find lawyers, and continuously updated the development of the case and contributed to online discussion. Deng was finally released without being charged under pressure from public opinion.[6]

Citizen journalists helped collect widespread concerns and suspicions from netizens about the earlier Yunnan hide-and-seek incident in 2009, in which a detainee was claimed to have died accidentally while he was playing a hide-and-seek game with other detainees in a prison. Another recent case is that of Lei Yang, an established young environmentalist with a master's degree from a prestigious university in China, who accidentally died while in custody on the suspicion of soliciting prostitution, which led to further investigation into the integrity in policing that may have been otherwise disregarded (Tatlow, 2016; Xinhua Net, 2009).[7] Citizen journalists were also the first to release information about the high-speed train collision incident in Wenzhou in 2011 online and continuously urged the government to conduct a thorough investigation and disclose the real causes of the accident to the public (Branigan, 2011).

Collective activism

More directly, the Internet works as a platform to initiate, organize, mobilize, and promote collective actions to shape particular policies or decisions, both online and offline. In 2009, the Chinese government planned to preinstall a mandatory content-control software called Green Dam Youth Escort in all personal computers sold in mainland China. Strong collective objections from domestic netizens as well as the international computer sector toward censorship forced the government to ultimately cancel the plan (BBC News, June 18, 2009; Koman, June 18, 2009). The parents of the victims of the 2008 melamin-tainted milk incident met on the Internet to exchange information and start a petition against the unreasonable government proposal for compensation (BBC News, November 10, 2010; The Telegraph, December 3, 2008).[8] The Internet also provided an efficient platform for netizens to question the responsibility of the government, relevant enterprises, and individuals, as well as the entire medical system in China, in the two significant vaccine scandals disclosed in 2010 and 2016, respectively (The Economist, April 1, 2016; Qian, 2010).[9]

Cancer-stricken college student Wei Zexi posted an online article in April 2016 that criticized the practice of Baidu, China's most popular search engine, for its pay-for-placement scheme on a promoted list of hospitals. He eventually died after a failed expensive medical treatment conducted by a Baidu-recommended hospital. Wei's case has triggered wide discussion and criticism of Baidu's advertisement policy and has led to an official probe into Baidu's management; Baidu's stocks significantly declined in the following month (Abkowitz and Chin, 2016; Ramzy, 2016). The Internet also helped organize spontaneous collective actions on the streets. A number of environmental protests against para-xylene (PX) chemical factories in multiple cities in the past decade or so were mostly mobilized and updated via the new social media (Hoffman and Sullivan, June 22, 2015).

These cases suggest that the Internet is politically consequential, at least in specific instances. However, applying the concept of the public sphere in the Internet is a stretch. The essential characteristics of the public sphere, according to Habermas, include rational exchange of ideas, respect of universal norms, and a unified sphere. The Internet is hardly a unified public sphere; idiosyncrasy dominates, and a single set of rules that all Chinese netizens respect and follow does not exist; netizens do not always engage in a rational exchange of views and opinions (Habermas, 2006; Marolt, 2011; Sullivan, 2012). By contrast, Chinese netizens are fragmented and divided into various chat rooms, which produce "a huge number of isolated issue publics" (Habermas, 2006, p. 423), and no opinion leaders are sufficiently influential to unite the majority of netizens. The millions of followers of the most popular microbloggers cannot account for a significant proportion of the more than 700 million Internet users (Marolt, 2011). In addition, Internet vigilantism and group-think have been observed. The former pertains to spontaneous online actions to monitor and punish others in the name of justice, and the latter refers to the tendency to agree upon extreme views within a group of like-minded people. Doxxing (*Renrou Sousuo* in Chinese, literally meaning human-flesh search) has become significant online collective activism against individuals who are believed to have engaged in unjust or immoral activities (Herold, 2011; Lagerkvist, 2010). Individual rights and privacy are often violated in these instances.

Carnival on the Internet

The Internet thus seems to be more likely a venue for a carnival than a town hall for deliberative assembly (Herold, 2011; Marolt, 2011). Bakhtin (1984) used the metaphor of a carnival as opposed to the official feast that referred to the activities matching the existing order and norms, to represent complete detachment from established institutions (i.e., social hierarchy and norms). People wearing costumes and masks in a carnival feel free from all the social tags and external pressure imposed on them, including surveillance by the state. Chinese Internet users further secure this sense when they believe that they are part of the hundreds of millions of ordinary Internet users and the probability of them being spotted by the police or state is minimal and that for punishment is even smaller. At a deindividuated state, "[w]hoever feels free is free" (Marolt, 2011, p. 58). Individuals tend to diminish self-regulation, act recklessly, and ignore supervision (Gilovich et al., 2006).

This argument particularly makes sense given the fact that most online activities are apolitical. Entertainment is the most popular activity engaged in by Internet users. According to the CNNIC data (July 2016), 55 percent of Chinese Internet users are online gamers and 72 percent are online shoppers. Even educated young people and university students seem more likely to devote their Internet time to recreation and personal networking rather than political discussion (Liu, 2011). Those engaged in online entertainment are less likely to have a chance to cross the line than those who participate in political deliberation. Supervision seems irrelevant to the former. Even the majority of university students that Liu (2011) interviewed did not think that they were censored and that censorship had anything to do with them (p. 170). Nevertheless, netizens cannot become irrelevant to the supervision and control of the state because of the following facts.

Varying control levels

The state's control and censorship over the Internet vary at different time points. "Upgrading" censorship and surveillance is usually a strong message to Internet users sent by the state intentionally. For instance, a series of campaigns to fight Internet crimes and suppress voices that challenged the political order and the legitimacy of the regime were launched in early 2013. These campaigns were reported extensively by the state media. Arresting big Vs – particularly Xue Manzi, a U.S. citizen and businessman with more than 12 million followers – became a salient event and was repeatedly reported by the China Central Television news (The Economist, August 29, 2013; Wang, 2013). Netizens are often reminded and are well aware of what the state can do.

Expanding the scope of political participation

In addition to policy and politics, activities in other fields may become politically relevant and participatory today. Bennett et al. (2012) point out "the politics of apolitical spaces" (p. 135) and suggest that activism that is seemingly irrelevant to politics may become political at the right moment. Norris (2002) proposes that the scope of political participation should be expanded to include "[a]ny dimensions of social activity that are either designed directly to influence government agencies and the policy process, or indirectly to impact civil society, or which attempt to alter systematic patterns of social behavior" (p. 16). Political participation should cover activities with regard to issues such as the environment, unemployment, public health, immigration, etc. Studies show that the Internet facilitates these activities (Liu, 2011; Livingstone et al., 2005).

For instance, the netizens' discussion about the 2011 Wenzhou high-speed train crash directly turned to the debate on whether quality was sacrificed in the quickly developed high-speed train system in China and whether abuse of power was the reason for the poor quality. Cases regarding food and vaccine safety and the environment, such as melamin-tainted milk, vaccine scandals, and anti-PX events, all concerned the state and became sensitive at times. Nationalistic sentiments tend to attract young netizens, which also concerns the state because nationalism may affect international relations and challenge the legitimacy of international policies of the state (Hyun et al., 2014; Zhao, 2005). Netizens have many opportunities to attract the state's attention, and they are unlikely to be left alone.

Positive propaganda

When the state realizes that mere surveillance, censorship, and deterrence are insufficient, it attempts to reckon on other lenient strategies, such as soft censorship. As of 2008, 280,000 Internet commentators financed and trained by the Chinese government attempted to direct and manipulate online discourse and engage in "positive propaganda" to defend the regime and the Party via techniques including mass posting of comments and simultaneously using numerous user accounts (Bandurski, 2008; Marolt, 2011; Stockmann and Gallagher, 2011).[10] One article from the *People's Daily*, the mouthpiece of the Chinese government, suggested embedding political indoctrination and education in online gaming and shopping (Guo, 2013). The soft power of the Chinese government will manifest in these seemingly politically irrelevant areas in the future. The difficulty for Internet users to achieve independence from the state in cyberspace will therefore continue to increase.

Illusory anonymity

An essential condition for the metaphor of carnival and the concept of deindividuation is that one believes that he or she is unlikely to be identified. However, becoming anonymous on the Internet is impossible. As early as 2003, users had to present their government ID cards when they went to Internet cafes. The real-name policy, where Internet users have to register their online accounts under their real names on the government ID cards, has been discussed, debated, and partially implemented (Chin, February 4, 2015). Cellphone users in China were then required to register their real names in 2015 (Zeng, September 2, 2015), and users must register their cellphone numbers to create online accounts, such as in Wechat, the most popular social networking application in China. Finally, a new cybersecurity law just passed in November 2016 mandated users of Internet services to register under their real names starting in June 2017.

Netizens cannot afford to ignore the state. Any Internet user who crosses the line can be persecuted. Shi Tao, a journalist, was sentenced to a 10-year imprisonment in 2005 because he disclosed a government document in an anonymous post to a U.S.-based website. Zhao Jing, a well-known political blogger under the name Michael Anti, believed that he was safe only because he was clearly aware of where the line was (Thompson, April 23, 2006). Thus, carnival does not exist on the Internet. Netizens can only stay anonymous to their fellow netizens, but not to the state. None of the metaphors can therefore represent the complexity of the Internet. The Internet lifts certain constraints on communication among netizens and promotes the exchange of ideas and dissemination of information, but it cannot emancipate netizens from the control imposed by the state. On the contrary, the Internet is a convenient means for the state to reach ordinary netizens. Rather than a panopticon, the public sphere, and carnival, the Internet acts like an exhibition hall that accommodates multiple venues, each containing separate sections. People discuss, debate, and deliberate "horizontally" with fellow netizens in chat rooms at one or more venues. At the same time, others, including the state, can read their views. The state also has one exhibition venue for presentation, and it promotes vertical interactions with netizens mainly through establishing e-government.

E-government

The state uses the Internet not only for taking control, but also for enhancing legitimacy (Herold, 2011; MacKinnon, 2011).

> Chinese government authorities have increasingly listened to Chinese netizens over the past few years, and they have opened channels of direct, online communication, ranging from occasional online chats between officials and netizens to the creation of websites that allow netizens to register complaints.
>
> (Herold, 2011, p. 206)

Thus far, e-government in comparative studies is not yet clearly defined. In general, it refers to "the electronic delivery of information from the government to citizens and between different government agencies" (Damm, 2006, p. 103). It often covers e-services and sometimes e-democracy. E-government is regarded as a means to boost government transparency, responsiveness, and accountability (Damm, 2006; West, 2001).

In China, the state encourages central and local government agencies to enable e-government functions. The launching of the Government Online Project at the end of the 1990s initiated the extensive development of e-government. The state encouraged the expansion of e-government in official documents and through annual evaluations of e-government performance of government agencies at the central and local levels since the mid-2000s.[11] As a preface to the series of political campaigns tightening up the control over the Internet since 2013, Xi's speech at the national propaganda and ideology work conference on August 19, 2013, clearly implied that the Chinese government would intensify the attempt to proactively take over cyberspace (Huang and Zhai, September 4, 2013). Only 145 government websites existed in 1998, but this number increased to 4,929 in 2002; the total number of websites with a suffix of "gov.cn" has reached 57,923 in 2015 (CNNIC, July 2002 and July 2015; Zhou, 2004). The Chinese government digitalizes official news and attempts to reinforce the official discourse in cyberspace. Administrative services are streamlined. How well administrative services are digitalized has become one of the new indicators for e-government evaluation. Apart from engaging in propaganda, disseminating information, and providing services, open government in cyberspace is also put on the agenda. Transparency of public information on the Internet has been emphasized in government documents.[12]

Interactive functions have been launched on government websites, allowing netizens to express their opinions and provide suggestions about public issues and policies. Through e-government, the state shows that it is open to and welcomes online reports of suspicious corrupt cases and suggestions from netizens. A function of *hudong*, which means "interaction," is displayed on the central government website and lists selected comments or suggestions from netizens and responses from relevant government agencies.[13] Local government websites also feature a subpage for public consultation, suggestions, and the contact information of local officials.[14] The website of *People's Daily* has one session of online surveys on salient issues. For instance, one of the survey questions asks people to identify the most serious problem in the Chinese government that requires an immediate action. The options include using public funds in private clubs, utilizing government vehicles for private use, reports full of official slogans, and empty promises. Raw statistics showed that half of the survey participants chose the last item as of June 24, 2016, indicating that Chinese officials were suffering a trust crisis.[15]

Other than official government websites, both individual government officials and government agencies have launched blogs and microblogs to appeal to the public. For example, a Weibo account (Chinese equivalent of Twitter) called "Safe Beijing" (*Ping'an* Beijing) is managed by the Beijing Municipal Public Security Bureau and has attracted millions of followers (Rubinstein, November 29, 2012).

These e-government functions present a hope to people that the state may take their suggestions seriously and listen to their complaints. Netizens may develop a sense that they are helping the government at the higher level bypass the lower-level government, thus avoiding the principal–agent problems, and listen to the grassroots movements. Thus, the interactive function shortens the psychological distance between the government and citizens. It nominally grants ordinary people who previously have no easy or direct access to government officials a chance to do so. Simply assuming that Premier Li Keqiang is reading one's comments on the other side of the wire may sufficiently make some people excited, politically efficacious, and thus supportive of the regime. This action probably reduces the degree of grievance and frustration that may otherwise push people to the streets and join the opposition. In the meantime, efficient administrative services and efforts for an open government via the Internet may further increase the legitimacy of the regime. After all, responsiveness and transparency are the supreme goal of a good government.

Dualism does not necessarily indicate square antagonism between the government and netizens, nor does it certainly entail a winner-take-all outcome. This book proposes that dualism remains relevant and is the central concept to understand the political effect of the Internet in China. The concept indicates that vertical communication between the government and netizens and horizontal communication among netizens are both politically consequential. To discuss the political influence of the Internet, this book particularly focuses on Internet exposure to such horizontal and vertical communications. The two forms of communication may yield either diverging or converging outcomes.

Internet exposure to horizontal and vertical communications

Chinese netizens tend to focus on politically tolerable and publicly resonant issues, thus creatively responding to state control (Esarey and Xiao, 2011; Yang, 2009). For example, they can challenge the regulations on migrant workers by condemning the beating and subsequent death of college graduate Sun Zhigang in Guangzhou (Tai, 2006; Tong and Lei, 2010) or fight corruption by investigating and disclosing the misconduct of a local official. Although straightforward and open deliberation of essential political issues may not be achieved in the near future in cyberspace, cyberdiscussion and cyberactions with respect to specific public affairs or issues may effectively cause changes in local leadership or policymaking.

Nevertheless, online content in China "reflects a compromise between what people want to say and what the regime is willing to permit them to say" (Esarey and Xiao, 2008, p. 771). The content a netizen is exposed to probably does not reflect the full spectrum of views among netizens. Internet commentators who are trained and hired by the state are also active participants in chat rooms. The job of these commentators is to guide and direct. Their comments and views may cloud horizontal communication. In addition, some bloggers and microbloggers are actually government officials who side with the state. Thus, horizontal communication is not always liberal.

In order for this pluralism of the Internet to become a systematic force for political liberalization, Chinese netizens have to overcome their intrinsic tendency of fragmentation pointed out by Habermas (2006) and avoid being dominated by a single source. Exposure to horizontal communication in multiple venues, such as bulletin board system (BBS) discussions, Wikipedia inputs, online news, or blogs or microblogs may reinforce pluralism and reduce the tendency of fragmentation and division among Chinese netizens.

Exposure to vertical communication, particularly via e-government, may boost one's positive attitude toward the current system, enhance regime support, and reduce antagonism against the state. However, propaganda and indoctrination embedded in e-government may bore netizens. The suggestions or reports made by netizens may not be responded to in an efficient or positive manner, which may become offensive. E-services may not be as efficient as expected. All these aspects can be potential factors counteracting the positive effect of E-government to the regime.

The political consequences of exposure to horizontal and vertical communications must be examined to speak to the political implications of the Internet. In particular, this book focuses on the effects of exposure to horizontal and vertical communications on political attitudes and behavior of the young elite in China. The structure of the book is as follows.

Chapter 2 introduces the subjects of this book: the educated youth in China. Political and socioeconomic characteristics of Chinese university students and the patterns in which they are exposed to the Internet are presented in this chapter. Their perceptions of the Internet from various perspectives are also introduced. Chapters 3, 4, and 5 explore the effects of Internet vertical and horizontal exposure on regime support and democratic values and resistance to political indoctrination and nationalism, respectively, based on statistical analyses of the survey data. The last chapter concludes the statistical analyses and discusses the new challenges and the political implications of cyberdualism in China.

Notes

1 For details of the rules of the pledge, see www.isc.org.cn/hyzl/hyzl/listinfo-15599. html and www.isc.org.cn/english/Specails/Self-regulation/listinfo-15321.html (for the English version), last accessed on November 20, 2016.
2 Some Chinese blogs also mentioned this news. For details, see http://zw.rbjfq. com/detail/lbr0m.html.

3 The most recent awardees are listed here: www.isc.org.cn/wzgg/listinfo-33742. html (for 2014–16); www.isc.org.cn/wzgg/listinfo-30227.html (for 2012–14); and www.isc.org.cn/hyjl/zghlwdh/listinfo-22461.html (for 2011–12), last accessed on November 20, 2016.

4 The document published by the Internet Society of China can be found at this link: www.isc.org.cn/hyzl/qyxypj/listinfo-13488.html, last accessed on November 20, 2016.

5 The list of Internet companies with their credit ratings for the first round can be found here: www.isc.org.cn/hyzl/qyxypj/listinfo-15701.html, last accessed on November 20, 2016.

6 A debate rose about whether the public opinion should affect the judicial process or not in China. See the two sides of this debate at: http://news.ifeng.com/opinion/society/200906/0616_6439_1205580.shtml and http://focus.cnhubei.com/local/200906/t712271.shtml, last accessed on November 20, 2016.

7 For details, see http://news.xinhuanet.com/english/2009-02/20/content_ 10855443.htm and www.nytimes.com/2016/05/13/world/asia/china-lei-yang-police-death.html?_r=0, last accessed on November 20, 2016.

8 Zhao Lianhai, a former employee of China's Food Quality and Safety Authority, the activist father of one of the victims in this case, founded a website called Home for Kidney Stone Babies (jieshibaobao.com结石宝宝之家) and organized parents through the website to take up a collective petition for reasonable compensation. The website was later blocked, and Zhao was sentenced two and a half years in prison because of "disturbing social order."

9 The relevant cases include the Shanxi vaccine scandal (2010) and China's vaccine scandal in 2016.

10 For details, please www.theguardian.com/technology/2005/jun/14/newmedia. china and www.scmp.com/news/china/policies-politics/article/1846729/police-china-set-stations-big-internet-website-firms, last accessed on November 20, 2016.

11 State Council of the People's Republic of China, *The State Council Circular on Further Strengthening the Management of Government Websites* ([2011] No. 40). To access the annual evaluation results in recent years, see www.mofcom. gov.cn/article/zt_jxpg2015/, last access on November 20, 2016.

12 For details, see 2015 年中国政府网站绩效评估 at www.mofcom.gov.cn/article/ zt_jxpg2015/lanmuone/201512/20151201198435.shtml, last accessed on November 20, 2016.

13 For details, see www.gov.cn/hudong/index.htm, last accessed on November 20, 2016.

14 For instance, see the Beijing government website: http://hudong.beijing.gov.cn/, last accessed on November 20, 2016.

15 For details, see http://71.people.com.cn/, last accessed on November 20, 2016.

References

Abkowitz, Alyssa and Josh Chin. May 2, 2016. China Launches Baidu Probe After the Death of a Student. *The Wall Street Journal*. Retrieved from www.wsj.com/articles/china-launches-baidu-probe-after-the-death-of-a-student-1462209685.

Bakhtin, Mikhail. 1984. *Rabelais and His World*. Bloomington, IN: Indiana University Press.

Bandurski, David. 2008. China's Guerrilla War for the Web. *China Media Project, HKU*. Retrieved from http://cmp.hku.hk/2008/07/07/1098/.

BBC News. June 18, 2009. China Clarifies Web Filter Plans. Retrieved from http://news.bbc.co.uk/2/hi/technology/8106526.stm.

BBC News. November 10, 2010. China Jails Tainted Milk Activist Zhao Lianhai. Retrieved from www.bbc.com/news/world-asia-pacific-11724323.

Bennett, Lance W., Deen G. Freelon, Muzammil M. Hussain, and Chris Wells. 2012. Digital Media and Youth Engagement. In *The Sage Handbook of Political Communication*, edited by Holli A. Semetko and Margaret Scammell. New York: Sage, pp. 127–140.

Brady, Anne-Marie. 2008. *Marketing Dictatorship: Propaganda and Thought Work in Contemporary China*. New York: Rowman and Littlefield Publishers.

Branigan, Tania. July 25, 2011. Chinese Anger Over Alleged Cover-Up of High-Speed Rail Crash. *The Guardian*. Retrieved from www.theguardian.com/world/2011/jul/25/chinese-rail-crash-cover-up-claims.

Chen, George, Charlie Smith, Steve Dickinson, David Schlesinger, Xiao Qiang, Rogier Creemers, and David Wertime. January 29, 2015. Is China's Internet Becoming an Intranet?: A China File Conversation. *China File*. Retrieved from www.chinafile.com/conversation/chinas-internet-becoming-intranet.

Chin, Josh. February 4, 2015. China Is Requiring People to Register Real Names for Some Internet Services: The Onus Is on Blogs, Instant-Messaging and Other Services to Implement Effective Tracking Systems. *The Wall Street Journal*. Retrieved from www.wsj.com/articles/china-to-enforce-real-name-registration-for-internet-users-1423033973.

China Internet Network Information Center (CNNIC). July 2002–July 2016. *The Statistical (Semiannual) Reports of Internet Development in China* (zhongguo hulian wangluo fazhan zhuangkuang tongji baogao). Retrieved from www.cnnic.cn/research/zx/qwfb/.

Damm, Jens. 2006. China's E-Policy: Examples of Local E-Government in Guangdong and Fujjian. In *Chinese Cyberspaces: Technological Changes and Political Effects*, edited by Jens Damm and Simona Thomas. London and New York: Routledge, pp. 102–131.

Dickie, Mure. February 18, 2006. China's Virtual Cops Pinpoint Web Dissent. *Financial Times*. Retrieved from www.ft.com/content/63d181a0-9fe6-11da-a703-0000779e2340.

Dou, Eva. August 5, 2015. China to Embed Internet Police in Tech Firms Cybercops Are Beijing's Latest Bid to Reduce Online Freedoms and Prevent "Spreading of Rumors". *The Wall Street Journal*. Retrieved from www.wsj.com/articles/china-to-embed-internet-police-in-tech-firms-1438755985.

Economist, The. August 29, 2013. Big Vs and Bottom Lines: Authorities Move Against Some of China's Most Vocal Microbloggers. Retrieved from www.economist.com/news/china/21584385-authorities-move-against-some-chinas-most-vocal-microbloggers-big-vs-and-bottom-lines.

Economist, The. April 1, 2016. A Vaccine Scandal in China Causes an Outcry. Retrieved from www.economist.com/news/china/21696166-latest-long-line-medical-abuses-reveals-widespread-corruption-dismal-lack.

Esarey, Ashley, and Qiang Xiao. 2008. Political Expression in the Chinese Blogosphere: Below the Radar. *Asian Survey*, 48(5), 752–772.

Fallows, James. 2008. The Connection Has Been Reset. *The Atlantic*. Retrieved from www.theatlantic.com/magazine/archive/2008/03/the-connection-has-been-reset/306650/.

Foucault, Michel. 1977. Discipline and Punish, Panopticism. In *Discipline & Punish: The Birth of the Prison*, edited by Alan Sheridan, pp. 195–228. New York: Vintage Books.

Gilovich, Thomas, Dacher Keltner, and Richard E. Nisbett. 2006. *Social Psychology*. New York: W.W. Norton & Company, Inc.

Griffiths, James. September 7, 2015. VPN Services Blocked in China as Astrill Warns of "Increased Censorship" Following WW2 Parade. *South China Morning Post*. Retrieved from www.scmp.com/tech/china-tech/article/1855964/vpn-services-blocked-china-astrill-warns-increased-censorship.

Guardian, The. July 16, 2002. Chinese Sites Agree to Censor Content. Retrieved from www.theguardian.com/technology/2002/jul/16/onlinesecurity. internetnews.

Guo, Mingfei. November 21, 2013. Combining Political Education and Online Gaming and Shopping. *People's Daily*. Retrieved from http://news.xinhuanet.com/politics/2013-11/21/c_125736289.htm （人民日报：把思想政治教育与网购网游相结合）.

Habermas, J. 1989. *The Structural Transformation of the Public Sphere: An Inquiry into a Category of Bourgeois Society*. Cambridge, MA: MIT Press.

Habermas, J. 2006. Political Communication in Media Society: Does Democracy Still Enjoy an Epistemic Dimension? The Impact of Normative Theory on Empirical Research. *Communication Theory*, 16, 411–426.

Herold, David K. 2011. Introduction: Noise, Spectacle, Politics: Carnival in Chinese Cyberspace. In *Online Society in China: Creating, Celebrating and Instrumentalising the Online Carnival*, edited by David Kurt Herold and Peter Marolt. New York: Routledge, pp. 1–20.

Higgins, Andrew. May 7, 2011. A Booze Blowout for China's Oil Giant. *Washington Post*. Retrieved from www.washingtonpost.com/world/asia-pacific/a-booze-blowout-for-chinas-oil-giant/2011/05/03/AFhXB67F_story.html.

Hoffman, Samantha and Jonathan Sullivan. June 22, 2015. Environmental Protests Expose Weakness in China's Leadership. *Forbes*. Retrieved from www.forbes.com/sites/forbesasia/2015/06/22/environmental-protests-expose-weakness-in-chinas-leadership/#2b4868302f09.

Huang, Cary and Keith Zhai. September 4, 2013. Xi Jinping Rallies Party for Propaganda War on Internet. *South China Morning Post*. Retrieved from www.scmp.com/news/china/article/1302857/president-xi-jinping-rallies-party-propaganda-war-internet.

Hyun, Ki Deuk, Jinhee Kim, and Shaojing Sun. 2014. News Use, Nationalism, and Internet Use Motivations as Predictors of Anti-Japanese Political Actions in China. *Asian Journal of Communication*, 24(6), 589–604.

Jacobs, Andrew. February 5, 2013. Chinese Blogger Thrives as Muckraker. *The New York Times*. Retrieved from www.nytimes.com/2013/02/06/world/asia/chinese-blogger-thrives-in-role-of-muckraker.html?pagewanted=all&_r=1.

Kalathil, Shanthi and Taylor C. Boas. 2003. *Open Networks Closed Regimes: The Impacts of the Internet on Authoritarian Rule*. Washington, DC: Carnegie Endowment For International Peace.

Koman, Richard. June 18, 2009. China's Not Backing Down But Green Dam Girl Fights Back. *ZDNet*. Retrieved from www.zdnet.com/article/chinas-not-backing-down-but-green-dam-girl-fights-back/.

Lagerkvist, Johan. 2010. *After the Internet, Before Democracy: Competing Norms in Chinese Media and Society*. New York: Peter Lang.

Lei, Ya-Wen. 2011. The Political Consequences of the Rise of the Internet: Political Beliefs and Practices of Chinese Netizens. *Political Communication*, 28, 291–322.

Liu, Fengshu. 2011. *Urban Youth in China: Modernity, the Internet and the Self*. New York: Routledge.

Livingstone, S., M. Bober, and E. J. Helsper. 2005. Active Participation or Just More Information? Young People's Take Up of Opportunities to Act and Interact on the Internet. *Information, Communication and Society*, 8(3), 287–314.

MacKinnon, Rebecca. 2007. Flatter World and Thicker Walls? Blogs, Censorship and Civic Discourse in China. *Public Choice*, 134(1–2), 31–46.

MacKinnon, Rebecca. 2011. China's "Networked Authoritarianism". *Journal of Democracy*, 22(2), 32–46.

McMullan, Thomas. July 23, 2015. What Does the Panopticon Mean in the Age of Digital Surveillance? *The Guardian*. Retrieved from www.theguardian.com/technology/2015/jul/23/panopticon-digital-surveillance-jeremy-bentham.

Marolt, Peter. 2011. Grassroots Agency in a Civil Sphere?: Rethinking Internet Control in China. In *Online Society in China: Creating, Celebrating and Instrumentalising the Online Carnival*, edited by David Kurt Herold and Peter Marolt. New York: Routledge, pp. 53–68.

Norris Pippa. 2002. *Democratic Phoenix: Reinventing Political Activism*. New York: Cambridge University Press.

Qian, Gang. March 26, 2010. We Must Know More About the Shanxi Vaccine Scandal. *China Media Project, HKU*. Retrieved from http://cmp.hku.hk/2010/03/26/5270/.

Ramzy, Austin. May 3, 2016. China Investigates Baidu After Student's Death From Cancer. *The New York Times*. Retrieved from www.nytimes.com/2016/05/04/world/asia/china-baidu-investigation-student-cancer.html?_r=0.

Rose, Adam and Andrew Roche. November 6, 2014. China to Clean Up "Harmful" Web Videos; Sites Pledge to Manage Online Comments. *Reuters*. Retrieved from www.reuters.com/article/us-china-internet-idUSKBN0IQ1LI20141106.

Rubinstein, Carl. November 29, 2012. China's Government Goes Digital. *The Atlantic*. Retrieved from www.theatlantic.com/international/archive/2012/11/chinas-government-goes-digital/265493/.

Stockmann, D. 2013. *Media Commercialization and Authoritarian Rule in China*. New York: Cambridge University Press.

Stockmann, D., and M. Gallagher. 2011. Remote Control: How the Media Sustain Authoritarian Rule in China. *Comparative Political Studies*, 44(4), 436–467.

Sullivan, Jonathan. 2012. A Tale of Two Microblogs in China. *Media, Culture & Society*, 34(6), 773–783.

Tai, Zixue. 2004. *Civil Society and Internet Revolutions in China*. Minneapolis: University of Minnesota Press.

Tai, Zixue. 2006. *The Internet in China: Cyberspace and Civil Society*. New York: Routledge.

Tang, Lijun and Yang Peidong. 2011. Symbolic Power and the Internet: The Power of a "Horse". *Media, Culture & Society*, 33(5), 675–691.

Tang, Lijun and Helen Sampson. 2012. The Interaction Between Mass Media and the Internet in Non-Democratic States: The Case of China. *Media, Culture & Society*, 34(4), 457–471.

Tang, Min and Narison Huhe. 2014. Alternative Framing: The Effect of the Internet on Political Support in Authoritarian China. *International Political Science Review*, 35(5), 559–576.

Tatlow, Didi Kirsten. May 12, 2016. Chinese Man's Death in Custody Prompts Suspicion of Police Brutality. *The New York Times*. Retrieved from www.nytimes.com/2016/05/13/world/asia/china-lei-yang-police-death.html?_r=0.

Telegraph, The. December 3, 2008. China Milk Scandal: Families of Sick Children Fight to Find Out True Scale of the Problem. Retrieved from www.telegraph.co.uk/news/worldnews/asia/china/3545733/China-milk-scandal-Families-of-sick-children-fight-to-find-out-true-scale-of-the-problem.html.

Thompson, Clive. April 23, 2006. Google's China Problem (and China's Google Problem). *New York Times Magazine*. Retrieved from www.nytimes.com/2006/04/23/magazine/23google.html.

Tong, Yanqi and Shaohua Lei. 2010. *Creating Public Opinion Pressure in China: Large-Scale Internet Protest*. EAI Background Brief No. 534, East Asian Institute, National University of Singapore.

Tong, Yanqi and Shaohua Lei. 2013. War of Position and Microblogging in China. *Journal of Contemporary China*, 22(80), 292–311.

Wang, Feng. August 25, 2013. Outspoken Chinese American Investor Charles Xue Detained in Beijing "Prostitution Bust". *South China Morning Post*. Retrieved from www.scmp.com/news/china-insider/article/1299448/outspoken-chinese-american-investor-charles-xue-detained-beijing.

Watts, Jonathan. June 14, 2005. China's Secret Internet Police Target Critics with Web of Propaganda. *The Guardian*. Retrieved from www.theguardian.com/technology/2005/jun/14/newmedia.china.

West, Darrell M. 2001. *State and Federal E-Government in the United States, 2001*. Online Article. Retrieved from www.insidepolitics.org/egovt01us.PDF.

Xiao, Qiang. August 29, 2010. Chinese Websites Establish "Self-discipline Commissioners." *China Digital Times*. Retrieved from http://chinadigitaltimes.net/2010/08/chinese-websites-establish-self-discipline-commissioners/.

Xiao, Qiang. 2011. The Battle for the Chinese Internet. *Journal of Democracy*, 22(2), 47–61.

Xinhua Net, The. February 20, 2009. China Netizens Join Probe into "Hide-and-Seek" Prison Death. Retrieved from http://news.xinhuanet.com/english/2009-02/20/content_10855443.htm.

Yang, Guobin. 2005. Environmental NGOs and Institutional Dynamics in China. *China Quarterly*, 181, 46–66.

Yang, Guobin. 2009. *The Power of the Internet in China: Citizen Activism Online.* New York: Columbia University Press.

Zeng, Vivienne. September 2, 2015. China Enforces Real-Name Registration for Phone User. *Hong Kong Free Press.* Retrieved from www.hongkongfp.com/2015/09/02/china-enforces-real-name-registration-for-phone-users/.

Zhao, Suisheng. 2005. China's Pragmatic Nationalism: Is It Manageable? *The Washington Quarterly*, 29(1), 131–144.

Zheng, Yongnian. 2008. *Technological Empowerment: The Internet, State, and Society in China.* Palo Alto, CA: Stanford University Press.

Zhou, Xiang. 2004. E-Government in China: A Content Analysis of National and Provincial Web Sites. *Journal of Computer-Mediated Communication*, 9(4). Retrieved from http://jcmc.indiana.edu/vol9/issue4/zhou.html.

Zhou, Xiang. 2009. The Political Blogosphere in China: A Content Analysis of the Blogs regarding the Dismissal of Shanghai Leader Chen Liangyu. *New Media and Society*, 11(6), 1003–1022.

2 Internet exposure of Chinese university students

Educated young netizens in China

Prior comparative evidence confirms that educated young people are more likely to use the Internet than other social groups (Norris and Inglehart, 2009; Scheufele and Nisbet, 2002) and spend more time with the Internet than other users (Shah et al., 2002). Web 2.0 technologies have also changed the features of political engagement, particularly among young generations worldwide (Bimber, 2012). Data from Western democracies confirm that young generations tend to depend on the Internet more than on traditional mass media – radio, print newspapers, and TV – for political information and that they are more likely to engage in online political communication than offline political participation (Bennett et al., 2012; Bimber, 2012). They utilize the Internet as an essential instrument to express their personal views with respect to public affairs. Recent statistics in China are consistent with these international observations.

Young Chinese comprise a substantial segment of Internet users. As of June 2016, more than half of the Internet users in China are younger than 30 (CNNIC, July 2016). By the end of 2015, more than 85 percent of young Chinese aged 25 or below are Internet users (CNNIC, August 2016). Thus, Internet penetration among Chinese youth is significantly higher than that among the overall Chinese population, which is approximately 52 percent (CNNIC, July 2016). Young people tend to depend on the Internet. Sixty percent of the young users aged 25 or below claim that they trust the Internet. Approximately 66 percent are willing to share on the Internet, and 49.2 percent are willing to post their comments digitally. More than 58 percent of this group reported themselves to be very or fairly Internet dependent (CNNIC, February 2015).

A university student user is even more involved with the Internet than an average young Chinese Internet user. Fifty-four percent of university student users are willing to comment on the Internet, and two-thirds report themselves to have developed Internet dependency (CNNIC, February 2015). Table 2.1 presents a list of major activity modes of online information

Table 2.1 Online information acquisition and communication of young Chinese Internet users

Internet Usage	Users in Secondary Schools	Users in Tertiary Schools	Nonstudent Young Users	Overall Young Users	Chinese Internet Using Population
Information Acquisition					
Search Engines	0.816	0.869	0.818	0.816	0.805
Online News	0.706	0.84	0.802	0.738	0.8
Blogs	0.179	0.245	0.173	0.176	0.168
Communication					
Instant Messaging	0.935	0.962	0.941	0.93	0.906
Microblog	0.459	0.606	0.442	0.444	0.384
Email	0.35	0.567	0.404	0.378	0.388
Forum/BBS	0.198	0.309	0.225	0.211	0.199

Source: Adapted from Table 2, CNNIC (February 2015)

Note: Each decimal in the table = the number of Internet users in each of the social categories (denoted by columns) who engage in each of the online activities (denoted by rows)/the total number of Internet users in that social category

acquisition and communication and the degrees in which students, nonstudents, and overall young user groups (aged 25 or below) engage in each activity compared with the total population using the Internet.

Overall, the table shows that tertiary school students who use the Internet score the highest in all the categories of information diffusion and communication activities compared with the total Chinese Internet users, overall young users, secondary school students, and nonstudent users. The results indicate that netizens obtain information online mainly via search engines and by reading news. Reading blogs contributes, but on a smaller scale. Approximately 87 percent of the Internet users in tertiary schools use online search engines, which is 5 percent or 6 percent higher than that in other groups. Eighty-four percent read online news, which is approximately 4 percent more than that in nonstudent users and the overall Chinese Internet users, and 10 percent more than that in overall young Internet users. University students who are Internet users are the largest consumers of online news. CNNIC data further show that more than 60 percent of Chinese university students who use the Internet read online news every day, which is greater than the 53 percent of the overall Internet youth who read online news every day (CNNIC, February 2015). Table 2.1 also indicates that approximately a quarter of tertiary school students who use the Internet rely on blogs for information, which is approximately 7 percent higher than the second largest group in the table.

The table further presents that tertiary school students are advanced users of online networking and communication instruments. More than 96 percent of the Internet-using students use instant messaging, and 60 percent utilize microblogs for communication. By contrast, only 46 percent or even less use microblogs in the other Internet-using groups. Tertiary school users are also likely to adopt email and online forums or use a BBS to communicate with others. More than 56 percent and 30 percent communicate via email and online forums or BBS, respectively, which are significantly higher than the rest of the categories. Educated youth maximize the use of Internet to acquire information and communicate with others.

This research concentrates particularly on university students, which comprise a digitally savvy segment of the Chinese population, and attempts to comprehend how the Internet affects Chinese people and the political system. To understand the effect of the Internet on Chinese university students, a survey was conducted from late 2010 to early 2011. The following section introduces the survey data and pattern of Internet usage among university students.

Sampling method and survey data

Two public universities were selected for the survey by adopting the stratified cluster sampling technique. One is a comprehensive university in Guangdong, and the other is a teaching university in Beijing. Both are ranked as key universities in China. A complete list of students in any public university is not accessible for sampling without official permission because of tight control over student registration in China. The current study utilized a convenient and plausible strategy to select a representative sample. All university students in China are required to reside in university dormitories for the purposes of centralized management (Ministry of Education, 2004). Thus, the full list of student dormitories is considered the sampling frame in the study. Sample dormitories were randomly selected in each of the two universities, and all the students living in the sample dormitories were included as survey respondents. Given the population sizes of the two universities, 102 dormitories were sampled from the normal teaching university and 216 from the comprehensive university; the response rates from the two universities were 82 percent and 87 percent, respectively. A total of 1,280 successful observations from university students were obtained.

The survey data capture the crucial political and socioeconomic features of today's university students, and some of these features become key explanatory variables in later chapters. The data also record the beliefs and values and evaluations of the students on the political influence of the

Internet. Important descriptive data are reported and discussed in the following sections.

Characteristics of university students in China

The characteristics of the educated youth greatly reflect the influences of the one-child policy, rapid economic development and globalization, advancement of information communications technologies, and a liberal social atmosphere (Liu, 2011). University students tend to be the center of family consumption, come from economically above-average urban families, and are Internet savvy; thus, they are comparatively informed. University students are more exposed to various sociopolitical experiences and are more individualistic than their parents are (Lagerkvist, 2010; Liu, 2011).

Aside from regularly conducting political indoctrination through state media and in classrooms, the party state particularly attempts to co-opt and control this group of future elite. They are administered closely online, as well as offline. Top universities were the earliest signees of the public pledge of self-regulation and professional ethics for China's Internet industry and engaged in strong self-regulation. University intranets can be arbitrarily blocked whenever the state or university administrators deem necessary, such as the shutdowns of Peking and Qinghua University intranets around the mid-2000s (Bregnbæk, 2016). Other indirect strategies are also adopted, such as charging a higher rate for Internet service that connects users to websites outside China than the university intranet service to dampen enthusiasm for the other side of the Great Firewall of China (Bao, April 22, 2013).

Political co-optation

The state attempts to recruit Chinese individuals into the Communist Party (CCP) and its affiliated organizations from the time they are children. School-age children are first recruited while they are in a primary school into the organization of Young Pioneers, which is administered by the Communist Youth League of China and under the leadership of the Party. When they enter secondary school and turn 14 years old, they are recruited into the Youth League. This practice becomes de facto, and almost every student must apply and join the Youth League when they reach 14, except for a small number of special cases, including those deemed as unqualified – for example, because of poor school performance and those who decided to defer. As high as 97.5 percent of the sampled university students joined the Youth League, whereas 2.5 percent, which are composed of 32 university students, did not.

University students are the future elite and "the core group of individuals who will play a pivotal role in China's transition and its future social, cultural, economic and political activities" (Liu, 2011, p. 1). The CCP has recently emphasized absorbing young talent into the Party and maintaining its legitimacy among the younger generation. The CCP begins recruiting students as early as in high school, but it recruits more students in universities. Students seem enthusiastic to become CCP members, and the competition to join the Party in universities is relatively high. After undergoing school-long political education, young students may sincerely believe in and join the Party. However, evidence suggests that state propaganda and political indoctrination can not function on those with high educational achievement in China (Chen and Shi, 2001; Kennedy, 2009; Rosen, 2003). Thus, voluntary party affiliation may be more of an outcome of personal cost–benefit calculations than a strong political belief because party membership is usually advantageous in the job market, particularly for secure and well-paid positions in the government and state-owned enterprises (Rosen, 2010a and 2010b; Saich, 2001).

Outstanding students tend to be recruited first unless they are unwilling to be co-opted. Official records indicate that 1.2 million university students became party members in 2010, which comprise 40.2 percent of the total CCP members recruited that year.[1] Party members account for 13.6 percent of this sample, which is significantly higher than the 7 percent national average.[2] Nine percent join the Party in high school, which confirms that the Party attempts to recruit young members immediately after they turn 18.

The parents of the educated youth are also overrepresented in the Party. Approximately 40 percent of the respondents come from families with at least one parent who is a CCP member. In particular, both parents of 11 percent of the students are CCP members. However, a simple chi-square test for independence indicates that the relationship between the respondent's party membership and that of his or her parents is statistically insignificant. No strong statistical evidence suggests that a relationship exists between parents' and their child's party affiliations.[3] Evidence suggests that party-member parents in China may encourage or discourage their child to join the Party (Bregnbæk, 2016).

Although university students may not sincerely believe in the Party, data show that they, similar to other Chinese social groups, generally express a positive attitude toward the Chinese government, particularly the central government. For instance, approximately 73 percent positively evaluate the performance of the central government in emergency management, particularly in handling the 2008 Sichuan Earthquake, which is much higher than the 47 percent who positively assess the local government in terms of emergency management. However, this hierarchical government trust may imply the unexpressed distrust toward the central government, which may lower the actual positive rating among this group (Li, 2016).

Socioeconomic advantages

University students are not only politically "advanced," but they have a strong socioeconomic background, too. They tend to come from wealthy urban families. The majority of these families are affiliated with state-owned enterprises.

The survey records the household registration status of the sampled students before entering university. More than 60 percent of the respondents possess an urban *hukou*. The students likely come from economically established families. This study uses living expenses to gauge the economic status of the respondents. Living expenses for full-time university students are primarily financed by their parents or other family members. University students may take part-time jobs and earn income irregularly. Nevertheless, regular financial support from one's family is considered an indicator of a respondent's economic status on two grounds. First, a part-time job while studying in a university is neither a stable source of income nor a reliable indicator of one's economic condition. Second, as a result of the one-child policy, university students of this generation tend to be the center of family expenses because they are the only children of their families (Liu, 2011). The provision of financial resources from parents to grown-up and working children is a common practice. Students in school are certainly sponsored mostly by their parents and families. Most families provide financial support to their children according to their children's needs and their own economic capacities. However, students from rich families may refuse financial support from parents and learn to be self-supporting, and some parents in financially moderate conditions may manage a life of austerity to provide a disproportionally high financial support to their children in universities. These cases are nevertheless not typical. Financial support from families can provide a valid and reliable proxy of the economic status of families and that of financially dependent university students.

The indicator included in the current study is the average, estimated, and monthly financial support from one's parents or other family members, which is exclusive of tuition or fees. The obtained monthly financial support of the sampled university students ranges from 0 to 6,500 yuan. Approximately 13 percent of the students receive an average of 300 yuan or less per month. Thirty-seven percent receive more than 300 yuan but less than 800 yuan. The rest (53 percent) receive 800 yuan or more. The per capita disposal monthly income of urban households in 2010, around the time of the survey, was approximately 1,592 yuan, half of which does

800 yuan account for, and that of rural households was only 493 yuan. Thus, the majority of the students must come from above-average families (China Statistical Yearbook, 2011).

The findings on the occupations of the students' parents are congruent with the earlier results. Both parents of more than a quarter of the respondents are working in the Party, military, government organizations, and other state-owned enterprises. Respondents who have one parent working in these areas account for as much as 45 percent. Jobs in these fields are comparatively secure and well paid. By contrast, only 16.4 percent of the respondents have one or both parents working in the agricultural sector, which is unprofitable.

Moreover, these students are likely exposed to international experiences. Overall, more than one-fifth of the students have gone abroad. These students have visited 38 countries and regions, covering Asian, African, North American, Australian, and European countries. However, the most frequently visited places remain located in Asia, particularly Hong Kong and Macau.

The political and socioeconomic backgrounds of university students imply that this group of educated youth tends to be the winners of the system or at least come from winning families. Do these factors make these students naturally close affiliates to the current regime? Does the "youth/subaltern norm" that "contests and questions the legitimacy of the elitist and hegemonic Party-state norm" dominate the students and make them defy the regime (Lagerkvist, 2010, p. 31)? The next three chapters include comprehensive analysis to answer these questions. Nevertheless, the following data suggest that this group of young people is politically attentive and willing to express their opposition on the streets.

Social and political activism

The data demonstrate that this sample of university students is socially engaged. They care for charity. Slightly less than two-thirds of this group participates in charity activities, including donation and volunteering. Students can easily organize associations in universities. Student associations tend to cover a large spectrum of topics and activities, from reading literature to music composition, environmental research to religious studies, and modern dancing to practicing martial arts. A total of 1,053 students, which comprise 82 percent of the sample, have participated in student associations in universities. Each student has, on average, 1.82 memberships, and as many as 30 percent have participated in three or more student associations.

This group of university students is sociopolitically well informed because of the development of information communications technology, particularly new media. Political awareness is regarded as correlated with political behavior (Zaller, 1992). The extant literature contends that Internet use and political awareness or interest are strongly associated (Anduiza et al., 2009; Boulianne, 2011). Public issues are often politically relevant. To measure the degree of public awareness of the sample, the respondents are asked if they know about any of the 13 salient instances that reflect profound political and social problems in China.[4] These instances have gained wide discussion on various media within the two years before the survey and cover a wide range of public issues.

The students are substantially exposed to and quite aware of these cases in general. Ten percent of respondents are aware of all 13 cases. The majority of the respondents, which accounts for 54 percent of the sample, identify between 6 and 10 cases. Only less than 2 percent of the respondents know about only one or no instance on the list.

In addition to strong social affiliations and great public awareness, many students have democratic experiences. Twenty-nine students, which comprise 2.3 percent of the sample, have voted in residents' committee elections or other community elections. Fifty, which account for approximately 4 percent, have voted in village elections. Forty, which comprise more than 3 percent of the sample, have even attended local people's congress elections. Thus, typical democratic activities, such as voting, are not completely foreign to this group of university students in China, particularly considering that approximately two-thirds of the sample has elected student leaders in classes or schools, and these electoral practices share some similarities with democratic procedures.[5]

Furthermore, university students do not hesitate to challenge authority and take to the streets. Approximately a quarter of the sample has participated in rallies or other collective actions for public expression. The survey question also documents the respondents' reflections in a hypothetical scenario, that is, "if you encounter unjust treatment in the university, what would you do?" Approximately 13 percent of the respondents would join a rally to articulate their concerns. Thus, at least a proportion of educated youth in China would follow the youth-subaltern norm rather than the party-state norm (Lagerkvist, 2010).

Exposure to horizontal and vertical communications in cyberspace

The Internet has greatly penetrated the lives of university students. The survey data reveal that new media have largely replaced old media instruments. More than 99 percent of the respondents in the sample surf online, whereas only one-fifth listen to the radio, 51 percent watch TV, and 75 percent read print newspapers on a regular basis. An average university student spends 0.09 hour daily listening to the radio, 0.36 hour reading print newspapers, 0.46 hour watching TV, and 2.9 hours using the Internet on a typical day. An average respondent has been surfing online for approximately seven years, excluding three invalid observations that indicate that the respondents began to use the Internet since he or she was born.[6] Thus, roughly one-third of one's life is associated with the Internet among this group. Moreover, university students engage in horizontal communication with other fellow netizens via different online platforms.

Online communities inside China first developed on university-based BBS forums (Yang, 2009a and 2009b). As of early 2008, 80 percent of Chinese websites hosted BBS forums, which attracted an average of more than 1 billion daily page views and 10 million new posts every day (Esarey and Xiao, 2008). Blogging and microblogging have rapidly expanded since the mid-2000s in China. As of June 2009, 181 million bloggers in China were managing more than 300 million blogs (CNNIC, July 2009). The number of microblogs in China reached 242 million as of June 2016 (CNNIC, July 2016). A university student is more involved in microblogging than an average Chinese Internet user. The most recent data show that one-third of the overall Chinese Internet users have microblogs, whereas 62 percent of Internet users in tertiary schools are microbloggers (CNNIC, August 2016). Another type of activity that involves a relatively small number of Internet users but is equally influential is web-encyclopedia input. Free online encyclopedias, such as the most popular Wikipedia or its Chinese counterpart Baidu Baike (Baidu encyclopedia), are open to the public. Web users can search the web encyclopedia without charge, and they can also input their points as they wish. Although an online encyclopedia provides more neutral and professional definitions than opinionated discussions, it is embedded with rich social and political meanings.

These students are extensively exposed to horizontal communications among netizens via blogs or microblogs, BBS forums, and Internet encyclopedias. They are both messengers and receivers of information. Approximately 60 percent of this sample has posted articles online via blogs or microblogs, which is consistent with the national figure. A total of 15.6 percent write about public affairs, 2.4 percent about financial and economic issues, more than a quarter about social problems, 5.6 percent about environmental issues, 12 percent about travel and shopping, more than 86 percent about life and relations, and 10 percent write novels online. Although the majority of bloggers or microbloggers focus on personal life, a certain number are concerned about public affairs and socioeconomic issues.

Blog viewers account for 77 percent of the sample. Forty-six percent of blog viewers are interested in public affairs, 15 percent in financial and economic issues, almost 60 percent in social problems, 12 percent in environmental issues, 21 percent in travel and shopping, more than 68 percent in life and relations, and 21 percent in novels. Overall, 72 percent of blog viewers are concerned with public affairs and issues in financial and economic and social and environmental arenas. Blog viewers seem to have a wide range of interests. The most popular blogger or microblogger is Han Han, a car racer and an opinion leader in current affairs (Strafella and Berg, 2015). Han Han's blog is identified as one of the three most viewed blogs by 161 students in the sample, which comprise more than 16 percent of the 984 blog viewers. Blog viewing among the sample seems quite diverse, and none aside from Han Han can attract a substantial proportion of university students. This finding also resonates Marolt's (2011) argument that netizens are quite divided and short of opinion leaders to effectively represent them and engage in fruitful deliberation.

Online forums/BBS constructs are another way for university students to acquire information and communicate with others. Approximately 70 percent of the respondents, which is composed of 880 students, have gone to online forums/BBS. This number is higher than the national figure of all students who use the Internet at the tertiary level reported by CNNIC in 2015 (see Table 2.1). More than one-third of this segment are interested in and read about public affairs, 12 percent about financial and economic issues, 45 percent about social problems, and 7.8 percent about environmental issues. A total of 58 percent of the respondents who go to BBS are concerned with public affairs and issues, which is higher than the 22.7 percent who are interested in travel and shopping, the 16 percent who read novels published on these websites, and the 42 percent who are interested in life and relations.

A total of 362 out of 880, which comprise 41 percent of the respondents who visit online forums or BBS, identify their university intranet forums as one of the three most visited online forums or BBS. Thus, the online activities of students can be closely monitored by university administrators and by the state via the school intranet. Aside from the university intranet, some private websites are also preferred by a certain number of students, including Tianya (n = 159, 18 percent of the 880 online forum goers), Baidu (n = 63, 7 percent), Mop (54, 6 percent), Renren (54, 6 percent), and Douban (27, 3 percent). This finding further confirms that Internet users scatter into various chat rooms, and a public sphere that attracts netizens for discussion and deliberation in cyberspace is lacking, except for the easily controlled university intranets.

Ninety percent of the students have been using web-encyclopedia to search information. More than 8 percent of the total sample has input their points to some online encyclopedia sites. Thus, web-encyclopedia also plays an important role in information dissemination. More than 40 percent of the respondents search on politics in some online encyclopedias; a quarter on finance and economy; approximately 19 percent on military; 57 percent on literature and science; 47 percent on culture, geography, and the environment; 52 percent on entertainment; 27 percent on travel; and two-thirds on important figures or celebrities. Of the 105 web-encyclopedia writers, 9.5 percent write on politics and 6.7 percent on finance/economy and the military, respectively; approximately a quarter on movies; 43 percent and 42 percent on literature and science, respectively; 30 percent on culture, geography, and the environment; another quarter on entertainment; 11 percent on travel; and 34 percent on important figures or celebrities. Netizens search web-encyclopedias for various issues, and the student contributors also write on a wide range of topics.

In addition to receiving information from fellow netizens, university students are significantly exposed to online news for information. Approximately three-quarters of the respondents have a habit of reading online news, which is slightly lower than the CNNIC 2015 figure that covers all tertiary-level students (see Table 2.1). Netizens have other ways to help disseminate information and promote horizontal communication, such as cross-posting. Cross-posting online articles written by others helps spread ideas and opinions instantaneously. Cross-posting can efficiently and effectively promote cyberexpression. Cross-posts, particularly in an image file format, can temporarily bypass state text-based censorship and counteract information control by attempting to make anything ever posted remain online longer than usual. The survey indicates that 18 percent of the sample respondents have cross-posted articles disclosing corruption and 39 percent have cross-posted articles related to social injustice.

Overall, horizontal information sources available to university students are diverse online. But not every student is open to this large spectrum of information sources. A number of university students stick to a limited number of venues for communication with fellow netizens. Vertical political communication in this study particularly refers to the voluntary communication between the state and netizens, as mainly promoted by e-government efforts. Netizens can choose to visit government websites, obtain government-disseminated news and information, and even interact with specific government officials. They can also choose to avoid e-government.

The survey data show that more than 46 percent of the students occasionally visit websites with a suffix of "gov.cn," and more than 2 percent are frequent or almost-every-day visitors. No reference point exists to indicate whether this group is actively involved in e-government. Considering that they are all university students and do not usually have to contact the government, such a contact rate is not trivial. University students visit government websites for multiple reasons. Forty-four percent of the visitors, which is composed of 260 students in this sample, attempt to learn more about public policies. Approximately one-third of the visitors look for information about government agencies or individual officials. Around one-quarter want to know the historical development of some localities. Approximately 3 percent (i.e., 16 subjects) visit official websites to contact local officials. More than one-quarter of the student visitors search government websites for research or study purposes.

Perceptions of the Internet

University students are highly exposed to horizontal and vertical communications online. Given their socioeconomic background and educational achievement, these students tend to be on the "right side" of the digital divide and become the significant beneficiaries of the advancement of information and communications technology and thus have a relatively positive attitude toward the overall effect of the Internet. Figure 2.1 includes multiple mini-charts that indicate the students' evaluations of the role of the Internet from various perspectives on a 5-point Likert scale. Mini-charts 1–3 and 7–11 are coded with "1" representing strongly disagreeing with the given statement and "5" indicating strongly agreeing with it. The rest of the mini-charts are coded as "1" if the respondent believes that the Internet greatly decreases his/her communication with different groups of people and "5" if he/she believes that the Internet greatly increases his/her communication with them.

The first six mini-charts capture a person's overall perceptions of the general role of the Internet. University students evaluate the Internet quite positively. More than 90 percent of the sample agree or strongly agree that the Internet increases work efficiency (mini-chart 1) and keeps one updated about current events and developments around the world (mini-chart 2). Relatively fewer people agree that the Internet is a good communication instrument. But still more than three-quarters in the sample perceive the Internet as useful in this aspect (mini-chart 3). Two-thirds of the students believe that the Internet promotes communication with family and friends (mini-chart 4). More than 70 percent assume that the Internet promotes communication with classmates or workmates (mini-chart 5) and those with whom they share the same hobbies (mini-chart 6).

Unlike the general evaluations of the Internet, slightly fewer people in this group affirm the positive role of the Internet in promoting political communication between the state and netizens and its influence to uphold a transparent and accountable government. However, these students still account for the majority of the sample. The university students believe that the Internet works as a platform for dialogue between netizens and the state. Slightly less than three-quarters agree or strongly agree that the Internet provides an opportunity for political expression (mini-chart 7),

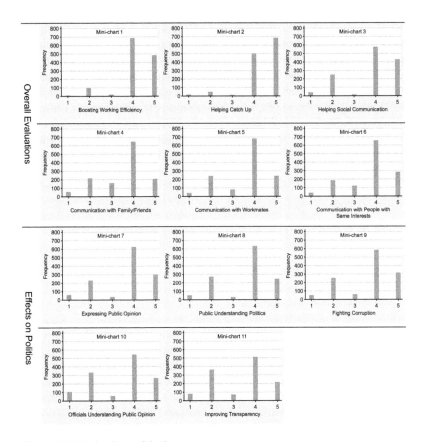

Figure 2.1 Evaluations of the Internet

Survey Questions:

Do you strongly agree, agree, stay neutral, disagree, or strongly disagree with the following statements?
Mini-chart 1: The Internet increases efficiency at work.
Mini-chart 2: The Internet keeps us updated with new developments and current events around the world.
Mini-chart 3: The Internet is a good means for social communication.
Mini-chart 7: The Internet grants an opportunity for political expression.
Mini-chart 8: The Internet helps the public understand politics.
Mini-chart 9: Reporting corrupt behavior online has become important to fight corruption.
Mini-chart 10: The Internet helps government officials understand the public opinion.
Mini-chart 11: The blogs or microblogs of government officials help build an open government.

Do you believe the Internet greatly increases, increases, brings no effects to, decreases or greatly decreases your communication with others?
Mini-chart 4: Your communication with your family and friends.
Mini-chart 5: Your communication with classmates or workmates.
Mini-chart 6: Your communication with those who share the same hobbies with you.

and 62 percent of these students agree or strongly agree that the Internet helps government officials understand the public opinion (mini-chart 10). Sixty-eight percent agree or strongly agree that launching the blogs or microblogs of government officials can help promote government transparency (mini-chart 11), and 71 percent agree or strongly agree that the Internet helps the public understand politics (mini-chart 8). Another 71 percent believe that the Internet plays a crucial role in combating corruption (mini-chart 9). Overall, university students strongly believe that the Internet promotes political communication between the state and netizens, thus probably improving the governance.

In conclusion, this group of educated young elite tend to come from socioeconomically well-performing families, which are likely affiliated with state-owned enterprises, and are the target of political co-optation. Nevertheless, these students are not easy to indoctrinate because they are socially active and politically aware. Some of them are not afraid to participate in collective actions for public expression. They are deeply embedded in the horizontal communication among netizens and take part in vertical communication with the state via the Internet. The majority strongly believe that the Internet is consequential in a variety of perspectives, including promoting political communication between the state and citizens and enhancing government responsiveness and transparency.

The following chapters focus on this group of university students and study specifically how their exposure to horizontal and vertical communications on the Internet shapes their democratic values and regime support, likelihood to resist to political indoctrination, and nationalism.

Notes

1 Data on student party membership are released by China Radio International. For details, see http://big5.cri.cn/gate/big5/gb1.cri.cn/33160/2011/07/01/23 05s3293758.htm, last accessed on November 20, 2016; 99 percent of tertiary-level institutions have their Communist Party committees (*China Education News*, July 1, 2011. See www.jyb.cn/, last accessed on November 20, 2016).
2 By the end of December 2015, the number of CCP members reached 88.7 million, accounting for approximately 6.8 percent of the total Chinese population. For details, see the 2015 report of the Organization Department of the CCP at http://news.12371.cn/2016/06/30/ARTI1467253408964468.shtml, last accessed on November 20, 2016.
3 Two chi-square tests have been conducted. In the first test, parents' party membership is coded dichotomously as "1" if any parent is a party member; as a result, Pearson chi2(1) = 0.7175, and Pr = 0.397. In the second test, parents' party membership is coded as "1" if one parent is a party member, "2" if both parents are members, and "0" otherwise; as a result, Pearson chi2(2) = 3.5185 and Pr = 0.172.

4 The 13 cases are the case of Zhang Haichao, who underwent a thoracotomy to defend his rights; the Yunnan hide-and-seek incident; the case of Deng Yujiao; the Green Dam incident; the tainted milk scandal; the black taxi entrapment scandal; the incident of Zhou Jiugeng; the incident of Sun Dongdong; the incident of Tang Fuzhen; cases of arrests outside the jurisdiction; corruption revealed in personal journals; incidents of toxic vaccine; and phony diplomas of celebrities.

5 For a visual presentation, watch the documentary *Please Vote for Me*, directed by Weijun CHEN. For an introduction, see: www.ln.edu.hk/ccs/resources/chidoc/pleasevote.pdf, last accessed on November 20, 2016.

6 The CNNIC's recent data demonstrate that the average time a student in the tertiary level uses the Internet has increased to 4.5 hours daily (CNNIC, August 2016). On one hand, the difference between the data used in this research and CNNIC data may be attributed to the actual increase in Internet use recently because of the proliferation of smartphones. On the other hand, this occurrence may be due to the fact that the subjects of this research are students in key universities instead of students in all tertiary schools.

References

Anduiza, E., A. Gallego, and L. Jorba. 2009. *The Political Knowledge Gap in the New Media Environment: Evidence from Spain*. Paper Prepared for the International Seminar Citizen Politics: Are the New Media Reshaping Political Engagement? Barcelona, 28–30 May.

Bao, Beibei. April 22, 2013. How Internet Censorship Is Curbing Innovation in China. *The Atlantic*. Retrieved from www.theatlantic.com/china/archive/2013/04/how-internet-censorship-is-curbing-innovation-in-china/275188/.

Bennett, Lance W., Deen G. Freelon, Muzammil M. Hussain and Chris Wells. 2012. Digital Media and Youth Engagement. In *The Sage Handbook of Political Communication*, edited by Holli A. Semetko and Margaret Scammell. London: Sage Publications Ltd, pp. 127–140.

Bimber, Bruce. 2012. Digital Media and Citizenship. In *The Sage Handbook of Political Communication*, edited by Holli A. Semetko and Margaret Scammell. London: Sage Publications Ltd, pp. 115–126.

Boulianne, S. 2011. Stimulating or Reinforcing Political Interest: Using Panel Data to Examine Reciprocal Effects Between News Media and Political Interest. *Political Communication*, 28, 147–162.

Bregnbæk, Susanne. 2016. *Fragile Elite: The Dilemmas of China's Top University Students*. Palo Alto, CA: Stanford University Press.

Chen, Xueyi, and Tianjian Shi. 2001. Media Effects on Political Confidence and Trust in the PRC in the Post-Tiananmen Period. *East Asia: An International Quarterly*, 19(3), 84–118.

China Internet Network Information Center (CNNIC). July 2002–July 2016. *The Statistical (Semiannual) Reports of Internet Development in China* (zhongguo hulian wangluo fazhan zhuangkuang tongji baogao). Retrieved from www.cnnic.cn/research/zx/qwfb/.

China Internet Network Information Center (CNNIC). Feburary 2015. *The Investigation Report of Chinese Juvenile Internet Using in 2014* (nian zhongguo qingshaonian shangwang xingwei diaocha baogao).

China Internet Network Information Center (CNNIC). August 2016. *The Investigation Report of Chinese Juvenile Internet Using in 2015* (nian zhongguo qingshaonian shangwang xingwei diaocha baogao).

China Statistical Yearbook. 2011. *National Bureau of Statistics of China.* Beijing: China Statistics Press.

Esarey, Ashley, and Qiang Xiao. 2008. Political Expression in the Chinese Blogosphere: Below the Radar. *Asian Survey*, 48(5), 752–772.

Kennedy, John J. 2009. Maintaining Popular Support for the Chinese Communist Party: The Influence of Education and the State-Controlled Media. *Political Studies*, 57(3), 517–536.

Lagerkvist, Johan. 2010. *After the Internet, Before Democracy: Competing Norms in Chinese Media and Society.* New York: Peter Lang.

Li, Lianjiang. 2016. Reassessing Trust in the Central Government: Evidence from Five National Surveys. *The China Quarterly*, 225(March), 100–121.

Liu, Fengshu. 2011. *Urban Youth in China: Modernity, the Internet and the Self.* New York: Routledge.

Marolt, Peter. 2011. Grassroots Agency in a Civil Sphere?: Rethinking Internet Control in China. In *Online Society in China: Creating, Celebrating and Instrumentalising the Online Carnival*, edited by David Kurt Herold and Peter Marolt. New York: Routledge, pp. 53–68.

Ministry of Education of the People's Republic of China, The. 2004. *The Ministry of Education Circular on Further Strengthening the Management of Student Dormitories in Higher Education Institutions* ([2004] No. 6).

Norris, Pippa and Ronald Inglehart. (2009). *Cosmopolitan Communications: Cultural Diversity in a Globalized World.* New York: Cambridge University Press.

Rosen, Stanley. 1993. The Effect of Post-4 June Re-Education Campaigns on Chinese Students. *The China Quarterly*, 134, 310–334.

Rosen, Stanley. 2010a. Chinese Youth and State-Society Relations. In *Chinese Politics: State, Society and the Market*, edited by P. H. Gries and G. Rosen. London and New York: Routledge, pp. 160–178.

Rosen, Stanley. 2010b. Is the Internet a Positive Force in the Development of Civil Society, a Public Sphere, and Democratization in China? *International Journal of Communication*, 4, 509–516.

Saich, Tony. 2001. *Governance and Politics of China.* New York: Palgrave.

Scheufele, Dietram, and Matthew C. Nisbet. 2002. Being a Citizen On-line: New Opportunities and Dead Ends. *The Harvard International Journal of Press/Politics*, 7(55), 55–74.

Shah, Dhavan, Michael Schmierbach, Joshua Hawkins, Rodolfo Espino, and Janet Donavan. (2002). Nonrecursive Models of Internet Use and Community Engagement: Questioning Whether Time Spent On-line Erodes Social Capital. *Journalism and Mass Communication Quarterly*, 79(4), 964–987.

Strafella, Giorgio and Daria Berg. 2015. The Making of an Online Celebrity: A Critical Analysis of Han Han's Blog. *China Information*, 29(3), 352–376.

Yang, Guobin. 2009a. *The Power of the Internet in China: Citizen Activism On-line.* New York: Columbia University Press.

Yang, Guobin. 2009b. On-Line Activism. *Journal of Democracy*, 20(3), 33–36.

Zaller, John R. 1992. *The Nature and Origins of Mass Opinion.* Cambridge: Cambridge University Press.

3 Internet exposure and political beliefs[*]

Introduction

The political effect of the Internet has been approached from various perspectives in both China and other countries, for example, from the perspectives of the quality of governance (Chadwick and May, 2003; Norris, 2004; Wong and Welch, 2004; Wu, 2009), political legitimacy (Kalathil and Boas, 2003), political engagement (Bennett et al., 2012; Mou et al., 2011; Yang, 2003), and political beliefs (Lei, 2011; Tolbert and Mossberger, 2006; West, 2004). Although previous studies have determined that the Internet has increased opportunities for interaction, these studies do not identify how the reliance of different kinds of users on one type of online information and communication source over another may affect outcomes.

This chapter specifically examines the relationship between Internet exposure and political beliefs. Comparative research argues that the Internet expands the public sphere by providing diversified information sources to enrich and deepen the horizontal political communication among ordinary netizens and suggests a positive relationship between Internet exposure and democratic beliefs (Balkin, 2004; Benkler, 2006; Dahlgren, 2000). Some specific studies in China support this finding and assert that Internet exposure breeds a critical-of-the-regime and democratically oriented public (Esarey and Xiao, 2011; Lei, 2011; Sullivan, 2012; Tang and Huhe, 2014; Tang and Sampson, 2012; Tang and Yang, 2011; Tong and Lei, 2013; Yang, 2005 and 2009; Zhou, 2009).

Other scholars warn that potentials and limitations coexist for the Internet to become a democratic space (Coleman and Blumler, 2012; Sullivan, 2012). Internet exposure cannot monotonically push for liberal values in China because strong state censorship and scrutiny may establish the Internet as a new arena for political propaganda (Kalathil and Boas, 2003; Shie, 2004; Zheng, 2008). Media instruments in authoritarian regimes, including the Internet, may increase regime support, as has been suggested in prior studies of government-controlled traditional media (Geddes and Zaller, 1989; Kennedy, 2009).

But empirical evidence implies that the Internet is less effective than traditional media instruments in indoctrinating its audience because of decentralization and diversification of digital information dissemination (Stockmann, 2013; Stockmann and Gallagher, 2011). One example of this pattern is found in the rapid development of e-government, which grants opportunities for citizens to voluntarily interact with the government. However, the effect of e-government instruments in Western democracies has been contradictory. Some empirical evidence suggests that e-government instruments have enhanced the interaction between citizens and government and therefore promoted the citizens' trust toward the government, whereas other studies do not (Morgeson et al., 2010; Tolbert and Mossberger, 2006; Welch et al., 2005; West, 2004).

This chapter addresses these debates about the influence of the Internet on political beliefs by analyzing two distinct forms of communication, namely, horizontal communication among netizens and vertical communication through e-government establishment. Empirical evidence from China suggests that horizontal communication, such as blogs, contains less propaganda, greater diversity, and more criticism of the regime than government-controlled and vertical media conversations (Esarey and Xiao, 2011; Sullivan, 2012; Tang and Huhe, 2014; Tang and Sampson, 2012; Tang and Yang, 2011; Tong and Lei, 2013; Yang, 2005 and 2009; Zhou, 2009). As a result, exposure to horizontal and vertical communications may distinctly influence one's political beliefs (Tang and Huhe, 2014). This chapter focuses on a person's democratic orientation and level of regime support. China's socialist regime is conventionally viewed as everything opposite of democracy, which makes one suppose that supporters for this regime automatically oppose democratic norms. Nevertheless, perceived dichotomy of democracy-versus-China is not evident because democracy is often mentioned in official discourse in China as a cure for power abuse and other problems in governance.

Previous work repeatedly finds that education mediates the extent to which exposure to political communication affects political beliefs. The most highly educated in authoritarian regimes are least influenced by exposure to government-controlled communication (Geddes and Zaller, 1989). Empirical findings in China also confirm that those with advanced education are less likely to be persuaded to support the regime (Kennedy, 2009). Hence, extant empirical studies suggest that media exposure to vertical government-led communication influences the highly educated the least. However, university students are the most deeply engaged group in cyberspace, as the data indicate in Chapter 2. The extent to which horizontal and vertical Internet exposure can influence the political beliefs of this particular group is an intriguing issue in research.

The civic culture

The civic culture particularly refers to a set of values and norms that underpin democracy (Almond and Verba, 1963). The civic culture emphasizes political engagement, respects civic rights and liberties, and features political efficacy, that is, self-confidence in understanding and participating in politics as an ordinary citizen. Previous literature confirms that Chinese netizens are more democratically oriented than non-netizens (Lei, 2011). This survey data document the level of civic culture among university students by recording their agreement levels with a series of statements capturing its key components. Mini-charts in Figure 3.1 specify the students' answers on a 5-point Likert scale, with "1" meaning strongly disagreeing with each statement and "5" indicating strongly agreeing. The data show that this group possesses rather strong civic values.

University students are very democratically oriented and emphasize engagement in the political process. More than 70 percent of the students in the sample agree or strongly agree with the statements highlighting popular election and political participation. Approximately 71 percent support the idea that competitive elections should become the major mode of political participation in China in the future (mini-chart 1), and 74 percent believe that local officials should be elected in a competitive election (mini-chart 4). Roughly the same number agree or strongly agree that students should proactively participate in politics (mini-chart 3). Eighty-two percent of the students believe that students, parents, and teachers should be allowed to participate in school management to promote fairness (mini-chart 2).

Even more people in this group assert that basic civil rights and freedoms, such as freedom of information and freedom of speech, should be guaranteed. Approximately 90 percent of the students agree or strongly agree that independent news media should be granted an opportunity for further development for freedom of information (mini-chart 5) and that everyone has freedom of speech regardless of one's attitudes or beliefs (mini-chart 6).

The majority is politically efficacious and confident in themselves in dealing with politics. Eighty-four percent disagree or strongly disagree with the statements that citizens should fully defer their rights and powers to capable and trustworthy leaders (mini-chart 8), and citizens do not play a role in governance and have to depend on the state (mini-chart 7). Seventy-one percent believe in equality between leaders and citizens and do not think that leaders should have any privileges (mini-chart 9). Thus, the survey data

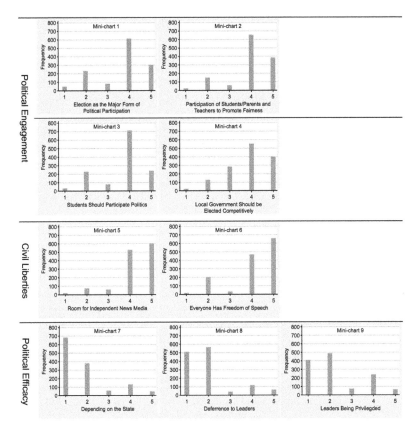

Figure 3.1 The civic culture among university students

Survey Questions:

Do you strongly agree, agree, stay neutral, disagree, or strongly disagree with the following statements?

Mini-chart 1: Elections should become the major form of political participation in China in the future.

Mini-chart 2: Allowing students, parents, and teachers to participate in school management contributes to fairness in education.

Mini-chart 3: Students should proactively participate in politics.

Mini-chart 4: Competitive elections should be used to elect local officials.

Mini-chart 5: Independent news media should be granted room for further development.

Mini-chart 6: Everyone has freedom of speech regardless of his or her attitudes or beliefs.

Mini-chart 7: The state and leaders are crucial for good governance, and ordinary citizens cannot play a role.

Mini-chart 8: Ordinary people do not need to participate in political decision-making if political leaders are competent and trustworthy.

Mini-chart 9: Government leaders deserve some privileges, for example, using government vehicles between home and work.

confirm that the civic culture is strong among university students. They tend to be democratically oriented and politically efficacious and believe in civil rights and freedoms.

Support of socialism

A high degree of civic culture does not necessarily indicate a low degree in regime support in China. Since the late 1990s, a high level of support for the regime has been frequently observed in China (Dickson et al., 2016; Kennedy, 2009; Li, 2004). The extant literature tends to measure regime support by recording the extent to which citizens self-reportedly trust, have confidence in, or are satisfied with government or leadership (Chen and Shi, 2001; Dickson et al., 2016; Kennedy, 2009; Li, 2004; Tolbert and Mossberger, 2006; Welch et al., 2005; West, 2004). This study instead documents one's attitudes toward the socialist ideology of the regime. The core components of socialism include the socialist political system, collectivism, and patriotism. Egalitarianism was one of the major components of the socialist framework promoted by the pre-Deng state, but it contradicted Deng's economy-dominated policies. Thus, egalitarianism was harshly criticized in post-reform political indoctrination and was left out in the post-Deng version of socialism. Patriotism was emphasized instead to enhance the legitimacy of the regime.

One may contend that these measures tend to attract politically correct answers. In a sense, any question that measures subjective feelings for the regime in an authoritarian system shares the same risk. Li (2016) asserts with solid evidence that survey measures of popular trust in the central government in China have been inflated. Chinese students have to take four compulsory and a number of elective courses for political education in high school, which are intended to promote their understandings of (and support for) the Marxist version of political economy, China's political system, and regime-sponsored values (Ministry of Education, 2004). Thus, asking politically inexperienced university students clearly defined items about the ruling ideology with which they have become familiar during the course of political education before coming to university is operationally more appropriate than asking them whether they generally trust or find the government to be satisfactory. They have a clear understanding of what they are being asked in the former case, and the upward bias in their answers is predictable.

University students who complete years of compulsory political education in school but are not given an opportunity for a reality check stick conveniently to answers in books, as demonstrated in Figure 3.2. The majority of them choose politically correct answers. Approximately 83 percent agree or strongly agree

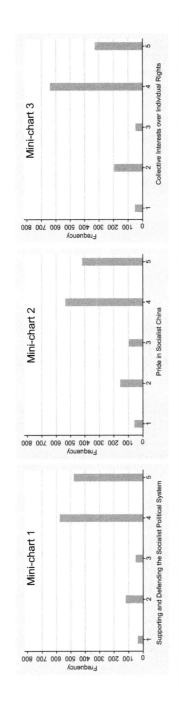

Figure 3.2 Support of socialism among university students

Survey Questions:

Do you strongly agree, agree, stay neutral, disagree, or strongly disagree with the following statements?
Mini-chart 1: We are obligated to support and defend the socialist political structure in our country.
Mini-chart 2: I feel proud of our socialist China.
Mini-chart 3: Sometimes individual rights have to give way to collective interests.

that ordinary citizens like themselves are obligated to support and defend the socialist political system, and 17 percent refuse to agree with the statement (mini-chart 1). Three-quarters feel proud of socialist China (mini-chart 2) and agree or strongly agree that sometimes individual rights have to give way to collective interest (mini-chart 3), whereas the rest do not.

Therefore, the data confirm that university students are both democratically oriented and supportive of the socialist ideology. Their answers to the set of statements with regard to socialism may be inflated. However, if the dependent variable increases by a constant term for all the observations, later regression results are not affected. It is thus believed that this universally upward change causes no systematic effect on the statistical results.

Measuring democratic orientation and regime support

Democratic orientation and support for the Socialist party state are latent constructs that cannot be directly measured. Instead, researchers can adopt observable indicators, such as self-reported attitudes and beliefs. In this chapter, one's attitudes toward the key components of the civic political culture and the socialist ideology are included in a principal component analysis (PCA) to examine the two latent concepts. Three of the statements reported in Figure 3.1 that determine one's attitudes toward political efficacy, electoral democracy, and civil liberties, respectively, are covered in the PCA.

> Statement 1: Ordinary people do not need to participate in political decision-making if political leaders are competent and trustworthy.
> Statement 2: Competitive elections should be used to elect local officials.
> Statement 3: Everyone has freedom of speech regardless of his or her attitudes or beliefs.

In the subsequent analysis, the answers to Statement 1 are reversely coded for consistency with the ascending trend of agreement with democratic norms reflected in the answers to the other two items. The three statements reported in Figure 3.2 that indicate one's levels of agreement with the three key components of socialist ideology, namely, the socialist political system, collectivism, and patriotism, are covered in the PCA.

> Statement 4: We are obligated to support and defend the socialist political structure in our country.
> Statement 5: I feel proud of our socialist China.
> Statement 6: Sometimes individual rights have to give way to collective interests.

Table 3.1 Principal component analysis loadings

Items	Regime Support	Democratic Orientation
Basic Democratic Norms		
S1. Ordinary people do not need to participate in political decision-making if political leaders are competent and trustworthy.	–0.1500	0.3982
S2. Competitive elections should be used to select local officials.	–0.0328	0.6184
S3. Everyone has the freedom of speech regardless of his or her attitudes or beliefs.	–0.0809	0.6622
Socialist Ideology		
S4. We are obligated to support and defend the socialist system in our country.	0.5938	0.1010
S5. I feel proud of our socialist China.	0.5979	0.0457
S6. Sometimes individual rights have to give way to collective interests.	0.5097	0.0909
Eigenvalues	2.19	1.53
% of common variance	0.3654	0.2542
Cumulative % of common variance (ρ) = 0.6195		

To construct uncorrelated latent variables of democratic orientation and regime support, a PCA based on the polychoric correlation is conducted. Polychoric correlation coefficients are estimated through a maximum likelihood procedure, assuming that the variables are latently continuous and normally distributed but observed by ordinal measures (Drasgow, 1988; Kolenikov and Angeles, 2009). Two factors are identified ($\rho = 0.62$) with their eigenvalues at 2.19 and 1.53, respectively. Table 3.1 reports the loadings of all six items on these two dimensions. According to the loadings, the first dimension is regime support and the second is democratic orientation. The aggregate measures of the two latent and dependent variables are computed based on the PCA results (Pearson's r = –0.0662). Subsequent sessions will be devoted to examining the extent to which Internet exposure shapes regime support and democratic orientation.

Four measures of exposure to online communication

Most previous studies rely on a single and often oversimplified measure for exposure to the Internet; these studies do not differentiate well among different types of usage. The ability to generalize is limited. For example, a dichotomous indicator is adopted in some literature to record whether one has ever been exposed to online communication in a general or a particular type of digital dialogue (Lei, 2011; Norris and Inglehart, 2009; Stockmann and Gallagher, 2011; Tolbert and Mossberger, 2006; West, 2004). However, people have a range of exposure. Some studies differentiate by asking about the frequency of exposure to determine the intensity of Internet use (Mou et al., 2011; Scheufele and Nisbet, 2002; Shah et al., 2002). Nevertheless, unless the source of what people read online is known, estimating the influence of Internet time on people's beliefs is difficult.

To probe the political consequences of Internet use in China, this study addresses the limitations of previous research by using multiple measures to capture the intensity, history, and nature of exposure to online communication. The study also goes beyond examining overall exposure to online communication to analyze online vertical communication between citizens and the government and horizontal communication among netizens.

Four specific aspects of exposure to online communication are incorporated. Internet use time and Internet age indicate the overall intensity and history of online communication. Two additional measures specify Internet exposure to vertical and horizontal political communications. The frequency of government website visits indicates the extent of the voluntary digital interactions of individuals with the government via the official e-government establishment. A set of four items that catalog different types of Internet venues, which one opens for information and ideas, is used to determine the degree of Internet exposure to pluralist horizontal political communication.

General Internet exposure: Internet time

The variable Internet time shows the intensity of general Internet exposure. The variable is measured in the research based on the average number of hours spent daily on the Internet. In this sample, Internet time extends from 0 to 18 hours daily. Mean time online is approximately 2.9 hours. Around 11 percent of the students spend, on average, less than one hour daily online, and one-quarter of them spend more than four hours per day surfing online.

General Internet exposure: Internet age

Time spent using the Internet suffices to describe a person's recent overall Internet exposure but not one's long-term involvement. The Internet kicks into one's life at different stages. Early exposure to online communication may shape an individual's political beliefs more than late Internet exposure. A person's earlier encounter with online communication before the launch of Web 2.0 in the late 1990s, however, was much less interactive than later Web 2.0 exposure. Thus, earlier years with the Internet may have yielded a trivial effect on political beliefs.

The variable Internet age in the data analysis indicates the number of years since the respondent first used the Internet and examines how experience affects political beliefs. Even though the subjects in the survey are young university students, the number of years since they first used the Internet varies between 1 and 16 years, with the mean value of around 7 years.[1] Six percent obtain only 1 or 2 years of exposure to online communication, whereas another 6 percent are digitally adept after having been exposed for more than 11 years.

Exposure to e-government

Comparative literature has tentatively suggested that e-government establishment is a strategy in a democratic system to promote trust toward the government (Tolbert and Mossberger, 2006; Welch, 2004). The role of e-government in China has not yet been systematically studied. In this book, the exposure to vertical communication via e-government will be captured based on the frequency of visiting websites with a suffix of "gov. cn." Table 3.2 demonstrates that the frequency of visiting e-government sites is coded incrementally on a 4-point scale with "1," "2," "3," and "4" meaning "never visited," "occasionally visited," "often visited," and "visited almost every day," respectively. The majority of university students, which comprise 51 percent (n = 655), have never visited any government websites. However, 595 students, or more than 46 percent of the sample, occasionally visit. A total of 26 students, which comprise 2 percent of the sample, often visit government websites, and 4 students visit these sites almost every day.

Table 3.2 Exposure to e-government

Frequency of Government Websites Visited	Observations	Percentages
Never (1)	655	51.17
Occasionally (2)	595	46.48
Often (3)	26	2.03
Almost every day (4)	4	0.31
Total	1,280	100

Exposure to pluralist horizontal information sources online

Habermas' (1989) critique of the Internet as the public sphere is that netizens are often divided into isolated public issue areas in separate chat rooms. Simultaneous exposure to multiple online information sources or venues is one way to counteract the tendency of fragmentation, maintain pluralism in cyberspace, and probably increase democratic orientation. Thus, this study documents the four types of online activities acquiring information about public issues and affairs, namely, reading news, searching a web encyclopedia, reading blogs or microblogs, and discussing on BBS forums. Each type of activity is coded dichotomously to capture horizontal Internet exposure. The blogs or microblogs of government officials are a part of e-government. Although netizens are likely aware that what they read is from an affiliate of the Chinese government, official bloggers initiate a conversation with netizens intentionally in a personal and nonhierarchical manner as an individual instead of as an institutionalized authority. Therefore, exposure to the blogs or microblogs of government officials is taken undifferentiatedly as one of the diverse sources in horizontal communication. In the meantime, communicating with government-affiliated commentators via these four horizontal venues cannot be differentiated from that with ordinary netizens either.

The survey data show that around three-quarters of the respondents routinely read news online; 57 percent read blog or microblog articles pertaining to public affairs and issues on financial and economic, social, and environmental issues; 40 percent discuss public affairs and issues on some BBS forums; and 60 percent search public issues and affairs with regard to politics, finance and economy, military development, culture, geography, and environment through a web encyclopedia. An additive index is generated to capture the degree of Internet exposure to horizontal political communication by specifying the number of the types of Internet venues that one opens for information and ideas. The results indicate that the exposure of an individual to horizontal political communication is significant among university students. Approximately half of the subjects have a score of "3" or "4." One-quarter have a score of "2," and 17 percent have a score of "1." The Internet is not a source for information or a venue for political communication for the remaining 9 percent of this sample with a score of "0."

The four aspects, namely, Internet time, Internet age, exposure to e-government, and exposure to horizontal information sources online, comprehensively describe Internet exposure to (political) communication.

Perceptions of the Internet

Statistical analysis based on a snapshot observation often suffers from the problem of endogeneity. For example, a person may argue that even if the variable of e-government visit exhibits a statistically significant effect on regime support, a *causal* effect cannot be confirmed because regime supporters tend to visit government websites in the first place. The extent to which visiting e-government sites increases one's support for the regime is difficult to extricate. Internet exposure may influence democratic orientation and regime support directly and indirectly. For example, if exposure to the Internet makes one *believe* that the Internet can help establish an open government via promoting vertical and horizontal communications, he or she may feel more positive about and therefore become supportive of the regime. To further examine the influence of Internet exposure, perceptions of the Internet as an intermediary platform to boost mutual understandings between netizens and government through vertical and horizontal communications are covered in the statistical analysis. The agreement levels of individuals with the following statements that have been discussed in Figure 2.1 in Chapter 2 are included in the later regression analysis.

> Statement 1: The Internet helps government officials understand public opinion.
> Statement 2: The blogs or microblogs of government officials help build an open government.

Traditional media

Some previous studies recognize the role of traditional media in China to promote regime support by exposing citizens to government-manipulated communication, but others do not (Brady, 2006; Chen and Shi, 2001; Kennedy, 2009; Li, 2004; Shambaugh, 2007; Stockmann and Gallagher, 2011). The survey data indicate that old media is not as penetrative as before and is certainly less influential than the new social media. Ninety-nine percent of the 1,280 university respondents surf online, whereas only 20 percent listen to the radio, 51 percent watch TV, and 75 percent read print newspapers. The three variables measuring the actual time spent with the three traditional media – radio, TV, and newspapers, respectively – are included in the regression models. The statistical analysis will illustrate whether old media still function to maintain regime support.

Control variables

Additional variables are controlled in the data analysis. Political and economic backgrounds and demographic features of the respondents are incorporated. University ID is controlled in the data analysis in case any systematic discrepancy exists in the political beliefs between students from the two universities. Family is the primary source for a child's political beliefs. The subjects in this study are full-time university students, and they may have never worked or lived outside school or their families (Glass et al., 1986). Thus, their parents' objective characteristics, that is, their party memberships and educational achievements, are controlled in the regression models.

Membership in the Chinese Communist Party (CCP)

Two mechanisms may increase regime support among party members. First, given the party-state political system in China, loyal party members sincerely support the party as well as the regime. Second, those who join the party for material interests and privileges are motivated to conceal their real motives and feel obligated to express their support for the party and the regime. By contrast, party membership does not constrain the expression of democratic orientation, and the terms of democracy, rights, and freedom often occur in official documents and speeches in China.

Financial support from family

The regular financial support from the family is captured in the regression models. The middle class is asserted to be the driving force for democracy. Thus, the quadratic term of this variable is incorporated into the data analysis in case of any curvilinear relationship between one's economic condition and political beliefs. In addition to the economic dimension, two more variables are used to measure the socioeconomic status and political affiliations of the respondents' parents to capture the other family influences.

Parents' political and socioeconomic backgrounds

Social reproduction theory contends that the parents' socioeconomic status is likely replicated by their children (Doob, 2013). The family is also proposed to play a primary role in political socialization and thereby shape children's political orientation (Glass et al., 1986). Parents' political status, which is measured by whether they are CCP members, and their educational achievements are recorded in the regression models. Each parent's educational attainment is measured categorically, with "1" meaning illiterate, "2" primary education, "3" junior secondary education, "4" occupational education, "5" senior secondary education, "6" associate degree, "7" bachelor's degree, and "8" postgraduate level or above. An index is created by combining the educational attainment levels of both parents. The variable of parents' political backgrounds adopts the same strategy. The variable is coded as "2" if both parents are Communist Party members at the time of the survey, "1" if one parent is, and "0" if neither is. Sixty percent have nonmember parents. Roughly 28 percent have one parent who is a party member. For the remaining 11 percent, both parents are party members.

The parents of the sample university students grew up before the deepening of economic reform and marketization, which was a period when market mechanisms had not yet dominated a person's life and the ideological stance of the party remained steadfast (Dickson, 2003; Saich, 2011). Compared to their children's generation, the parents had joined the party more likely because of political beliefs than for economic calculations. Thus, they may have transferred their political beliefs and values to their children to some extent. The party memberships of the parents may have helped maintain their children's regime support. On the contrary, educated parents may encourage their children to be more critical and resistant to political indoctrination.

Level of institutional control

University ID is controlled to capture the consequences of institutional features, if any. Students are sampled from one normal teaching university and one comprehensive university. Students from the normal teaching university may be more supportive of the regime because of the heavy teaching of ethics and institutional control imposed on them.

Demographic characteristics of age and gender are also controlled. Detailed summaries of all the variables are listed in the appendix.

Data analysis and results

The dependent variables are aggregate and continuous measures. Thus, ordinary least squares (OLS) models are used for data analysis. Natural log transformation is applied to the dependent variables to make the data more normally distributed. To correct standard errors and reduce bias in estimation, survey design effects are controlled for with the universities as strata and dormitories as primary sampling units, and observations are weighted by sampling probabilities and response rates computed for their respective universities. Variance inflation factors are computed for the independent variables, all of which remain less than or equal to 1.79, which suggests the absence of a multicollinearity problem (Belsley et al., 1980). Regression results from the four models are reported in Table 3.3. Models 1 and 2

Table 3.3 OLS regression results controlled for survey design effects and sampling probabilities

	Model 1: DV = ln (Support for the Socialist Regime)		Model 2: DV = ln (Support for the Socialist Regime)		Model 3: DV = ln (Democratic Orientation)		Model 4: DV = ln (Democratic Orientation)	
	B	Std. Err.	B	Std. Err.	B	Std. Err.	B	Std. Err.
Internet Exposure								
Exposure to government websites	0.044	0.018*	0.044	0.018*	-0.023	0.013	-0.023	0.013
Exposure to horizontal communication	-0.012	0.008	-0.012	0.008	0.023	0.006***	0.023	0.006***
Internet age	-0.002	0.003	-0.002	0.003	0.002	0.002	0.002	0.002
Internet time	-0.007	0.006	-0.007	0.006	-0.001	0.003	-0.001	0.003
Perceptions of Intermediary Internet between Government and Citizens								
Internet helping officials understand the public opinion	0.015	0.008	0.015	0.008	0.005	0.006	0.005	0.006
Officials' blogs helping build an open government	0.023	0.010*	0.023	0.010*	0.013	0.006*	0.013	0.006*
Exposure to Traditional Media								
Newspaper time	0.028	0.016	0.028	0.016	-0.010	0.014	-0.010	0.014
TV time	0.020	0.010*	0.020	0.010*	0.005	0.007	0.005	0.007
Radio time	0.014	0.040	0.013	0.040	0.025	0.023	0.026	0.023

Control Variables

CCP membership	0.060	0.029*	0.059	0.029*	0.018	0.016	0.019	0.016
Economic background	-0.037	0.019	-0.064	0.029*	0.008	0.011	0.026	0.020
Economic background (square term)	–	–	0.010	0.006	–	–	-0.006	0.004
Parents' educational attainments	-0.005	0.003	-0.005	0.003	-0.001	0.002	-0.001	0.002
Parents' party memberships	-0.008	0.017	-0.008	0.017	0.005	0.011	0.005	0.011
University ID (teaching = 1)	0.015	0.018	0.012	0.018	-0.019	0.011	-0.017	0.011
Gender (male = 1)	-0.089	0.021***	-0.091	0.021***	-0.045	0.013***	-0.045	0.013***
Age	-0.023	0.008**	-0.023	0.008**	-0.009	0.005	-0.009	0.005
_cons	2.314	0.158***	2.336	0.158***	2.053	0.101***	2.039	0.102***
Number of strata		2		2		2		2
Number of PSUs		317		317		317		317
Number of obs.		1162		1162		1162		1162
Population size		1381926		1381926		1381926		1381926
Design df		315		315		315		315
F statistic		5.2 (16, 300)		4.92 (17, 299)		3.05 (16, 300)		2.92 (17, 299)
Prob > F		0.0000		0.0000		0.0001		0.0001
R-squared		0.1172		0.1182		0.0705		0.0714

Note: *$p \leq 0.05$; **$p \leq 0.01$; ***$p \leq 0.001$

examine regime support, and Models 3 and 4 analyze democratic orientation. Models 2 and 4 contain the quadratic term of family financial support.

The political influence of the Internet

The results across all four models demonstrate that the Internet influences political beliefs through exposure to specific vertical and horizontal political communications. Government web visitors are significantly more supportive of the regime. The negative correlation between exposure to vertical communication and democratic orientation has nearly passed the threshold for statistical significance ($p = 0.06$ in Models 3 and 4). For each level increase in the frequency of government web visits, the score of regime support rises by approximately 4.4 percent and that of democratic orientation decreases by roughly 2.3 percent. By contrast, exposure to horizontal political communication through digital venues is significantly associated with a belief in basic democratic norms but has no statistically significant effect on regime support. The score of democratic orientation rises by around 2.3 percent for a one-level increase in horizontal exposure.

Although confirming an interactive relationship per se contributes to "the larger picture of digital media in politics," causation cannot be confirmed (Bimber, 2012). Even though the temporal priority of causality is met in the sense that political beliefs are measured at the time of the survey and exposure to online political communication is measured by the past experiences of subjects, additional information is required to determine whether the correlations observed in the data analysis are causal. However, panel data are not available to examine the longitudinal influence of e-government establishment on political beliefs over time.

Nevertheless, the perceptions of the intermediary role of the Internet between government and netizens in vertical and horizontal communications may help further elucidate this issue. The agreement level with the statement that the blogs or microblogs of government officials can help build an open government is positively and statistically significantly associated with regime support. A person's view with the statement that government officials can have a better understanding of public opinion through the Internet is also correlated with regime support on a reasonable significance level ($p < 0.07$ in Models 1 and 2). Thus, those who perceive that the Internet successfully improves government inclusiveness and transparency portray the Chinese government more positively and therefore become more supportive of it. For each agreement level increase with the statements, the scores of regime support rise by 2.3 percent and 1.5 percent, respectively, in Models 1 and 2. Hence, both Internet exposure and positive perceptions of exposure to digital political communication enhance regime support.

The perception on the blogs or microblogs of officials is also positively associated with democratic orientation. Those who recognize that the Internet, especially the blogs or microblogs of government officials, provides opportunities for netizens to know more about both officials and the policy process and hence contributes to open government tend to be more democratically oriented. For each agreement level increase with the statement, the scores of democratic orientation rise by 1.3 percent in both Models 3 and 4. This correlation is not straightforward. On one hand, a democratically oriented person may be more likely to recognize democracy from Internet exposure. On the other hand, witnessing democratic practices may be useful to develop a strong democratic orientation.

Neither Internet age nor time of Internet use imposes any statistically or substantively significant influence on the dependent variables. Thus, general Internet exposure does not affect political beliefs when the specific exposure to political communication is controlled. The early years of exposure to Web 1.0 do not contribute to the development of democratic orientation or help enhance regime support. The failure of overall Internet exposure time to shape political beliefs is consistent with the previous findings that a distinctive amount of time is actually spent on politically inconsequential activities (Norris and Inglehart, 2009; Shah et al., 2002).

Traditional media

The statistical results show that the time spent on TV promotes regime support. Time spent on newspapers also has a positive effect on regime support on a relatively statistically significant level (p = 0.08) in both models. For each additional daily hour spent on TV, the scores of regime support increase by 2 percent in both Models 1 and 2. For each additional daily hour spent on print newspapers, the scores of regime support rise by 2.8 percent in both models. Thus statistically, traditional media instruments still function to maintain the legitimacy of the party-state among the Chinese-educated young elite in this digital age. Nevertheless, considering that the average daily time spent with TV and newspapers is 0.46 hour and 0.36 hour, respectively, one daily hour increase is difficult to acquire for a typical university student today. Thus, the actual effect of traditional media may not be that salient. Traditional media does not influence democratic values of this group of young Chinese.

Political and economic backgrounds

The results in Table 3.3 illustrate that the political backgrounds and economic conditions of the Chinese university students are statistically associated with regime support but not with democratic orientation. A party member is likely to express his or her support for China's regime. The results in Models 1 and 2 indicate that a party member's score for regime support is 6 percent and 5.9 percent, respectively, higher than that of a nonmember. He or she may support the regime sincerely out of loyalty to a party and the regime or expressively out of obligation. However, party membership does not statistically influence democratic orientation. Thus, a party member tends to be as democratically or undemocratically oriented as a nonmember. For ordinary Chinese citizens, China's regime does not intrinsically contradict a democratic system. Hence, supporting the regime and the Party in China does not necessarily mean rejecting democracy. A party member may express his or her strong support for the regime and believe in democratic norms at the same time.

The economic status of financially dependent university students is inherited from their families. For the sake of demonstration, the variable of family financial support to a subject is normalized by its mean in the data analysis. The factor is not associated with democratic orientation, but it reduces regime support. The regression results in Model 2 indicate that economic status is negatively associated with support for the regime at a 0.025 level of statistical significance. However, the quadratic term does not pass the 0.05 level of statistical significance. Therefore, the U-shaped relationship is not confirmed. In fact, the coefficient of this factor in Model 1, where no quadratic term is included, is also close to the 0.05 level of statistical significance (p = 0.058). Hence, the variables of financial support from family and regime support likely have a linear negative relationship, although the trend declines at the end. However, a robust U-shaped relationship cannot be identified. The results in Model 1 indicate that for every additional mean value increase in financial support sent from family to the university student, which is roughly 778 RMB, the score of his or her regime support drops by approximately 3.7 percent.

Parents' political and socioeconomic backgrounds

Other than economic conditions, parents and family do not significantly influence the political beliefs of university students. The educational attainment and party affiliations of parents do not shape their children's political values and beliefs probably, because the higher education obtained by university students overcomes any political influences from their parents.

Level of institutional control and demographic features

The regression results demonstrate that the coefficients of the variable of university ID do not pass the threshold of statistical significance of 0.05. But this variable demonstrates a rather statistically significant effect (p = 0.08) in Model 3, suggesting that students in the normal teaching university are less agreeable with basic democratic norms about political participation, civil liberties, and electoral democracy than their counterparts in the other university. Holding other factors constant, a student from the normal teaching university has, on average, a score for democratic orientation around 1.9 percent lower than his or her counterpart in the comprehensive university, according to the results in Model 3. Two potential sources cause this systematic difference in political beliefs among students between the two universities. The first may be attributed to the students' self-selection. A normal teaching university may have attracted students from poor families because of its low tuition and subsidies to students. The discussion on economic background in the previous section suggests that they tend to be more supportive of the regime than their richer counterparts. However, their economic backgrounds do not influence democratic orientation. Statistical tests comparing the group means of students from the two universities also yield no significant results for monthly financial support from family.[2] Moreover, this factor and other potentially influential individual characteristics, including the political and socioeconomic characteristics of students and their parents, are all controlled in the data analysis.

Thus, the difference in democratic orientation between students from the two universities may probably be attributed to institutional and environmental factors. The institutional control in a normal teaching university is generally high, and ethics and political responsibility have been emphasized. The liberal atmosphere in Guangdong may instead breed a democratic orientation for university students. Hence, students in the normal teaching university in Beijing become either less liberal or more cautious about expressing their democratic values. As a result, at a less significant but still robust level, this discrepancy at the institutional level likely shapes the expressed democratic orientation of university students.

Demographic features, such as age and gender, exhibit a statistically significant influence on political beliefs. Males tend to refuse to support the regime and also reject democratic norms. So do older students, only on a less significant level. The coefficients of age in Models 3 and 4 do not pass the 0.05 threshold of statistical significance, but these coefficients are still relatively robust (p = 0.058 in Model 3 and p = 0.065 in Model 4). The findings suggest that male and older students tend to be conservative in expressing their attitudes toward the regime and democratic norms and avoid choosing extremely positive answers to the survey questions. They demonstrate the same tendency for regime support and democratic values, and the substantive effects appear greater on regime support than on democratic orientation (8.9 percent and 9.1 percent in Models 1 and 2 vs. 4.5 percent in Models

3 and 4 for the variable of gender and 2.3 percent in Models 1 and 2 vs. 0.9 percent in Models 3 and 4 for the variable of age). Thus, their answers are unlikely the results of political pressure and sensitive questions. The moderate answers of older male students probably reflect their true political beliefs. The findings confirm that regime support and democratic orientation in the students' perceptions do not necessarily contradict each other. Those who do not strongly support the current regime are not necessarily democracy-seekers. Individuals who believe in basic democratic norms do not necessarily challenge the current regime.

Conclusion

This chapter examines the extent to which exposure to digital communication affects the political beliefs of Chinese university students. By focusing on two types of political beliefs, namely, regime support and democratic orientation, this study adopts multiple measures of the degree of exposure to digital communication and differentiates between vertical political dialog between citizens and the government through the establishment of e-government and horizontal political discussion among individual netizens. The findings suggest that the Internet affects political beliefs.

Visitors to government websites in China are more supportive of the regime and less democratically oriented than others. The positive perceptions of the Internet as an intermediary platform to enhance mutual understandings between government officials and netizens also boost regime support. The Internet helps the Chinese government not only by increasing exposure to e-government, but also by promoting an image of open government. By contrast, those exposed to pluralistic horizontal online information sources agree more with the basic democratic norms than others. A belief that the blogs or microblogs of government officials can promote an open government is also positively correlated with democratic orientation. Therefore, both actual Internet exposure and beliefs in the influence of Internet exposure on governance simultaneously shape a person's views about the regime and democracy.

Another interesting finding casts strong doubt on the conventional view that the refutation of the party state in China parallels the demand for democracy. The contrast between the relationships of exposure to the two specific types of online political communication with the dependent variables does not imply that the two types of political beliefs completely contradict each other in the perceptions of this group of highly educated young Chinese. Exposure to horizontal communication increases democratic orientation, but no statistical evidence indicates that it decreases regime support. Older male university students who are not very supportive of the regime are also doubtful about the basic democratic norms. Communist Party members are obligated to express their support for the regime, but they are not necessarily less democratically oriented than the rest. At least among educated youth in China, the dichotomy of China versus democracy is not what they have perceived. One may support the regime out of loyalty or obligation and simultaneously believe in the core democratic norms and enthusiastically hope that China can move in that direction. By contrast, one may dislike the regime and continue to disagree with democratic norms.

Notes

* This chapter is derived from an article published in *Journal of Contemporary China* on 24 April 2014, available online: www.tandfonline.com/10.1080/106705 64.2014.898903.
1 Three additional observations recorded Internet age roughly equal to the respondents' ages. These three observations were omitted from data analysis to avoid any outlier-induced bias.
2 T-score = 0.3 (p = 0.78 for the two-tailed test) for the test of financial support from family between students from the two universities; unequal variances for the two groups are assumed.

References

Almond, Gabriel A. and Sidney Verba. 1963. *The Civic Culture: Political Attitudes and Democracy in Five Nations*. Thousand Oaks, CA: Sage Publications, Inc.

Balkin, Jack M. 2004. Digital Speech and Democratic Culture: A Theory of Freedom of Expression for the Information Society. *New York University Law Review*, 79, 1–5.

Belsley, David A., Edwin Kuh, and Roy E. Welsch. 1980. *Regression Diagnostics: Identifying Influential Data and Sources of Collinearity*. New York: John Wiley and Sons.

Benkler, Yochai. 2006. *The Wealth of Networks: How Social Production Transforms Markets and Freedom*. New Haven, CT: Yale University Press.

Bennett, Lance W., Deen Freelon, Muzammil Hussain, and Chris Wells. 2012. Digital Media and Youth Engagement. In *The Sage Handbook of Political Communication*, edited by Holli A. Semetko and Margaret Scammell. London, UK: Sage, pp. 127–140.

Bimber, Bruce. 2012. Digital Media and Citizenship. In *The Sage Handbook of Political Communication*, edited by Holli A. Semetko and Margaret Scammell, p. 118. London, UK: Sage.

Brady, Anne-Marie. 2008. *Marketing Dictatorship: Propaganda and Thought Work in Contemporary China*. New York: Rowman and Littlefield Publishers.

Chadwick, Andrew and Christopher May. 2003. Interaction Between States and Citizens in the Age of the Internet: "E-Government" in the United States, Britain, and the European Union. *Governance*, 16(2), 271–300.

Chen, Xueyi and Tianjian Shi. 2001. Media Effects on Political Confidence and Trust in the PRC in the Post-Tiananmen Period. *East Asia: An International Quarterly*, 19(3), 84–118.

Coleman, Stephen and Jay Blumler. 2012. The Internet and Citizenship: Democratic Opportunity or More of the Same? In *The Sage Handbook of Political Communication*, edited by Holli A. Semetko and Margaret Scammell. London, UK: Sage, pp. 141–152.

Dahlgren, Peter. 2000. The Internet and the Democratization of Civic Culture. *Political Communication*, 17, 335–340.

Dickson, Bruce. 2003. *Red Capitalists in China: The Party, Private Entrepreneurs, and Prospects for Political Change*. Cambridge, NY: Cambridge University Press.

Dickson, Bruce J., Mingming Shen, and Jie Yan. 2016. Generating Regime Support in Contemporary China: Legitimation and the Local Legitimacy Deficit. *Modern China*, 43(2), 123–155.

Doob, Christopher B. 2013. *Social Inequality and Social Stratification in US Society*. Upper Saddle River, NJ: Pearson Education, Inc.

Drasgow, Fritz. 1988. Polychoric and Polyserial Correlations. In *Encyclopedia of Statistical Sciences*, Vol. 7, edited by L. Kotz and N. L. Johnson, pp. 69–74. New York: Wiley.

Esarey, Ashley and Xiao Qiang. 2011. Digital Communication and Political Change in China. *International Journal of Communication*, 5, 298–319.

Geddes Barbara and John Zaller. 1989. Sources of Support for Authoritarian Regimes. *American Journal of Political Science*, 33(2), 319–347.

Glass, Jennifer, Vern L. Bengtson, and Charlotte Chorn Dunham. 1986. Attitude Similarity in Three Generational Families: Socialization, Status Inheritance, or Reciprocal Influence? *American Sociological Review*, 51(October), 685–698.

Habermas, Jürgen. 1989. *The Structural Transformation of the Public Sphere: An Inquiry into a Category of Bourgeois Society*. Cambridge, MA: MIT Press.

Kalathil, Shanthi and Taylor C. Boas. 2003. *Open Networks, Closed Regimes: The Impact of the Internet on Authoritarian Rule*. Washington, DC: Carnegie Endowment for International Peace.

Kennedy, John James. 2009. Maintaining Popular Support for the Chinese Communist Party: The Influence of Education and the State-Controlled Media. *Political Studies*, 57, 517–536.

Kolenikov, Stanislav and Gustavo Angeles. 2009. Socioeconomic Status Measurement with Discrete Proxy Variables: Is Principal Component Analysis a Reliable Answer? *The Review of Income and Wealth*, 55(1), 128–165.

Lei, Ya-Wen. 2011. The Political Consequences of the Rise of the Internet: Political Beliefs and Practices of Chinese Netizens. *Political Communication*, 28(3), 291–322.

Li, Lianjiang. 2004. Political Trust in Rural China. *Modern China*, 30(2), 228–258.

Li, Lianjiang. 2016. Reassessing Trust in the Central Government: Evidence From Five National Surveys. *The China Quarterly*, 225, 100–121.

Ministry of Education of the People's Republic of China, The. 2004. *Putong Gaozhong Sixiang Zhengzhi Kecheng Biaozhun (Siyan)* (Standards for Courses on Ideology and Politics in High School (provisional)) ([2004] No. 5).

Morgeson, Forrest V. III, David VanAmburg, and Sunil Mithas. 2010. Misplaced Trust? Exploring the Structure of the E-Government-Citizen Trust Relationship. *Journal of Public Administration Research and Theory*, 21, 257–283.

Mou, Yi, David Atkin, and Hanlong Fu. 2011. Predicting Political Discussion in a Censored Virtual Environment. *Political Communication*, 28(3), 341–356.

Norris, Pippa. 2004. *Deepening Democracy via E-Government*. Draft Chapter for the UN World Public Sector Report. Retrieved from www.hks.harvard.edu/fs/pnorris/Acrobat/World%20Public%20Sector%20Report.pdf.

Norris, Pippa and R. Inglehart. 2009. *Cosmopolitan Communications: Cultural Diversity in a Globalized World*. New York: Cambridge University Press.

Saich, Tony. 2011. *Governance and Politics of China*. London: Palgrave Macmillan.

Scheufele, Dietram and Matthew C. Nisbet. 2002. Being a Citizen On-line: New Opportunities and Dead Ends. *The Harvard International Journal of Press/Politics*, 7(55), 55–74.

Shah, Dhavan, Michael Schmierbach, Joshua Hawkins, Rodolfo Espino, and Janet Donavan. 2002. Nonrecursive Models of Internet Use and Community Engagement: Questioning Whether Time Spent On-line Erodes Social Capital. *Journalism and Mass Communication Quarterly*, 79(4), 964–987.

Shambaugh, David. 2007. China's Propaganda System: Institutions, Processes and Efficacy. *The China Journal*, 57, 25–58.

Shie, Tamara Renee. 2004. The Tangled Web: Does the Internet Offer Promise or Peril for the Chinese Communist Party? *Journal of Contemporary China*, 13(40), 523–540.

Stockmann, Daniela. 2013. *Media Commercialization and Authoritarian Rule in China*. New York: Cambridge University Press.

Stockmann, Daniela and Mary E. Gallagher. 2011. Remote Control: How the Media Sustains Authoritarian Rule in China. *Comparative Political Studies*, 44(4), 436–467.

Sullivan, Jonathan. 2012. A Tale of Two Microblogs in China. *Media, Culture & Society*, 34(6), 773–783.

Tang, Lijun and Helen Sampson. 2012. The Interaction Between Mass Media and the Internet in Non-Democratic States: The Case of China. *Media, Culture & Society*, 34(4), 457–471.

Tang, Lijun and Peidong Yang. 2011. Symbolic Power and the Internet: The Power of a "Horse". *Media, Culture & Society*, 33(5), 675–691.

Tang, Min and Narison Huhe. 2014. Alternative Framing: The Effect of the Internet on Political Support in Authoritarian China. *International Political Science Review*, 35(5), 559–576.

Tolbert, Caroline J. and Karen Mossberger. 2006. The Effects of e-government on Trust and Confidence in Government. *Public Administration Review*, 66(3), 354–369.

Tong, Yanqi and Shaohua Lei. 2013. War of Position and Microblogging in China. *Journal of Contemporary China*, 22(80), 292–311.

Welch, Eric W., Charles C. Hinnant, and M. Jae Moon. 2005. Linking Citizen Satisfaction with E-Government and Trust in Government. *Journal of Public Administration Research and Theory*, 15, 371–391.

West, Darrell M. 2004. e-government and the Transformation of Service Delivery and Citizen Attitudes. *Public Administration Review*, 64(1), 15–27.

Wong, Wilson and Eric Welch. 2004. Does E-Government Promote Accountability? A Comparative Analysis of Website Openness and government Accountability. *Governance*, 17(2), 275–297.

Wu, Guoguang. 2009. In the Name of Good Governance: E-Government, Internet Pornography, and Political Censorship in China. In *China's Information and Communications Technology Revolution: Social Changes and State Responses*, edited by Xiaoling Zhang and Yongnian Zheng, pp. 68–85. New York: Routledge.

Yang, Guobin 2003. The Internet and Civil Society in China: A Preliminary Assessment. *Journal of Contemporary China*, 12(36), 453–475.

Yang Guobin. 2005. Environmental NGOs and Institutional Dynamics in China. *China Quarterly*, 181, 46–66.

Yang, Guobin. 2009. *The Power of the Internet in China: Citizen Activism Online*. New York: Columbia University Press.

Zheng, Yongnian. 2008. *Technological Empowerment: The Internet, State and Society in China*. Stanford, CA: Stanford University Press.

Zhou, Xiang. 2009. The Political Blogosphere in China: A Content Analysis of the Blogs regarding the Dismissal of Shanghai Leader Chen Liangyu. *New Media and Society*, 11(6), 1003–1022.

4 Internet exposure and political resistance

Introduction

Chapter 3 confirms that Internet exposure to e-government can enhance regime support. One explanation is that the Chinese government utilizes the Internet to provide e-information, e-services, and seemingly e-democracy by proactively accepting suggestions and comments from the digital public. As a result, an ordinary netizen may believe that the government attempts to increase transparency and responsiveness and become supportive of the regime. Nevertheless, another strategy of the Chinese government by using the Internet may also contribute to regime support; this strategy is political propaganda (Kalathil and Boas, 2003; Zheng, 2008). Political propaganda reinforces ruling ideologies and provides a rationale for the regime. Aside from teaching rigid doctrines repeatedly, the Chinese government adopts "positive propaganda" and indoctrinates through "soft" strategies, such as storytelling (Stockmann and Gallagher, 2011).

The extant literature approaches political propaganda in China either by mapping out the structure of the propaganda system (Brady, 2006; Shambaugh, 2007) and examining the content of political indoctrination (Fairbrother, 2004) or by analyzing trust in political institutions and regime legitimacy as the outcome of propaganda (Chen and Shi, 2001; Fairbrother, 2003 and 2008; Kennedy, 2009; Rosen, 1993; Stockmann and Gallagher, 2011). However, the studies focusing on the supply side cannot determine the effectiveness of the propaganda apparatus on a target audience. Research exploring the other end of the propaganda system has only inferred the influence of political indoctrination from the degree of self-reported political trust and regime support and has failed to measure its actual influence on citizens. The extant literature generally disregards the agency of citizens in the process of political indoctrination. However, citizens may actually obtain some autonomy to escape from political teaching, and their cooperation is critical to explain the effectiveness of political propaganda. Thus, instead of focusing on the reported regime support, this study attempts to capture a more immediate response to propaganda, which is resistance to political education among Chinese university students.

Resistance may not be always demonstrated in a blatant action. Individuals who are not convinced of government-controlled communication may not publicly deny it in a repressive system. Nevertheless, citizens may resist in a subtle and uncontentious manner when it is tolerated by the government. Resistance in this study refers to James Scott's (1985) "everyday forms of resistance." Ordinary citizens engage in daily, passive, and individualistic resistance to a hegemonic process executed by the state. Although this measure may still possibly underestimate the real level of disagreement, uncontentious resistance in a behavioral form is a more accurate and tangible alternative to self-reported political trust and regime support.

The formal education system has been one of the major media for political propaganda.[1] State-constructed political education programs in school have been established since the late 1950s under the rule of the Chinese Communist Party (CCP) to maintain state legitimacy and national cohesion (Fairbrother, 2004). Curriculum and textbooks of political teaching are centrally designed for elementary, secondary, and tertiary education, and the implementation of political education is supervised by the Central Propaganda Department of the CCP and the Ministry of Education ([2005] No. 5). In elementary and secondary schools where attendance in each class is closely monitored by teachers and regularly updated with parents, young students do not have substantial leeway to skip any class, including those that teach political principles. However, students in most universities have obtained significantly more freedom to choose whether to attend any class than their elementary and secondary counterparts. Absence, especially from general education (GE) courses, including political education, is pervasive and widely tolerated. Frequent absences indicate lack of interest and noncompliance. This chapter considers absence from political education as an indicator of resistance to political indoctrination and studies the extent to which Internet exposure contributes to the resistance of university students in the process of political teaching.

Media constructs another medium for political propaganda. Traditional media – TV, radio, and newspapers – have played an important role in maintaining regime legitimacy (Baum, 2008; Geddes and Zaller, 1989; Kennedy, 2009;). The Internet is significantly more commercialized and substantially less controlled by the state than traditional media instruments ever since China was digitally connected. The state has to self-restrain from directly intervening in the management of the new media sector and depend on indirect regulatory means to control online communication (Stockmann, 2013). Although the current Xi-Li administration recently initiated the restructuring of Internet governance to tighten up control over the Internet, online communication has become irreversibly individualistic and diversified. Dominant pluralism on the Internet squarely contradicts any political doctrine. Empirical evidence from China implies that the Internet is less effective than traditional media instruments in producing a positive view about political institutions even through "positive propaganda" (Stockmann and Gallagher, 2011, Table 4.1, p. 455). Some previous studies and Chapter 3 in this book confirm that Internet exposure promotes a democratic culture and engenders politically sophisticated netizens, and hence counteracts state propaganda attempts (Balkin, 2004; Benkler, 2006; Dahlgren, 2000; Esarey and Xiao, 2011; Lei, 2011; Sullivan, 2012; Tang and Huhe, 2014; Tang and Sampson, 2012; Tang and Yang, 2011; Taubman, 1998; Tong and Lei, 2013; Yang, 2003, 2009a and 2009b; Zhou, 2009).

However, e-government may function as a political tool to indoctrinate ordinary Internet users (Brady, 2006 and 2008; Kalathil, 2002; Kalathil and Boas, 2003; MacKinnon, 2007 and 2011; Zheng, 2008). E-government began to be promoted at national and local levels almost once the country was connected to the Internet, and e-government facilities have been rapidly developed since the end of the 1990s. Premier Li Ke Qiang highlighted the concept of "Internet +" in his 2015 Government Work Report and called for efforts to build China into a "strong Internet country," which signaled a greater degree of future government involvement in cyberspace than before. Cyberspace provides a platform for the government to reinforce the official interpretation of history and current events to advocate the ruling ideologies and sustain regime legitimacy. However, the findings in Chapter 3 suggest that the statistically significant effect of Internet exposure to vertical communication on regime support may largely be attributed to a person's belief that the Internet helps build an open and responsive government and not digital propaganda. Nonetheless, the "propaganda 2.0" is presented in a format that greatly appeals to the Internet-savvy generation, and thus may reduce resistance to political education (The Economist, December 13, 2014).

Internet exposure may yield divergent results on political resistance, as was demonstrated in the last chapter. On one hand, exposure to digital pluralism helps engender liberal citizenship and may therefore increase the level of resistance to political indoctrination. On the other hand, it may promote support for authoritarianism through e-government and probably obedience toward political teaching. The following sections of this chapter examine these hypotheses.

Resistance to political indoctrination among university students

University students are required to take certain general education courses, including a series of lessons teaching the ruling ideologies, in the name of political thoughts and theories (Pang, 2010; Propaganda Department and Ministry of Education, 2005). Absence from courses on political education in universities is considered an indicator of resistance to political indoctrination on the following grounds. First, as mentioned earlier, students in university have much more autonomy to control their own schedules, and professors are less vigilant and more tolerant to absences in universities, particularly from GE courses. Students feel little pressure to skip those courses. Some students in this sample even explain their absence from political teaching based on the absence of other individuals.

Second, the basic ideas discussed in the courses on political education have already been delivered prior to university and therefore are mostly redundant, which rules out the possibility for students to attend merely to learn. Redundancy appears in students' answers as one of the reasons for being absent. Third, absence does not affect grade or performance. Teaching and examination in political education closely follow the centrally designed textbooks and guidelines. In fact, some students mention in the survey that memorizing the information in textbooks is more efficient than listening to teachers to pass the final examination, and attendance is seldom checked or computed into the final grade. Students commonly admit that the classes are boring, impractical, and dogmatic (see Table 4.2). Under such circumstances, attendance in these inconsequential and time-wasting classes can be regarded as a form of compliance, and absence a form of uncontentious resistance.

One may expect the resistance to political indoctrination to be greater among the well educated than among the poorly educated. Higher education may reduce the level of compliance in state propaganda by promoting citizenry and increasing the political sophistication of students. Empirical findings confirm that exposure to political indoctrination does not change the political attitudes of the most educated individuals in authoritarian regimes (Geddes and Zaller, 1989). Empirical data in China also illustrate that exposure to state-manipulated communication only increases regime support of rural residents with lower educational achievement; no systematic effect has been found on those who are highly educated (Kennedy, 2009). Re-education efforts in Chinese universities after the 1989 Tiananmen Square movement did not successfully restore regime-sponsored values (Rosen, 1993). Education is found in some studies to be negatively related to political trust (Chen and Shi, 2001). Thus, behavioral resistance to political education may not be rare in this group of subjects, and a reasonable variation can be observed for analysis.

Absence from political education is indeed pervasive in Chinese universities according to the survey. Although underreport is not very likely, the survey questions are designed to reduce sensitivity, if any. Before the questions are asked, a statement is formulated to help the subjects reflect on this issue and ensure them that skipping compulsory GE courses is a quite common practice of many students in a university. The subjects are asked to describe the general picture of absence in their classes. After that, his or her own experiences of skipping are asked. The first question reads, "We all have experiences of skipping classes in university. According to your observation, on which subject(s) do the general education classes have a lowest turnout?" A list of subjects is provided, including advanced mathematics, basics in computer science, English or foreign languages, physical education, military theories, and political education. A follow-up question is asked, "From which of the above subjects have you been mostly absent?" Students are allowed to choose three subjects at most. Table 4.1 summarizes the results.

The first column in Table 4.1 reports the respondents' estimation of the most unpopular GE courses. Physical education, advanced mathematics, and second languages are comparatively popular among university students and absence rates are relatively low, according to students' estimation. Among 1,280 undergraduate students, 2.6 percent point out that physical education (PE) is among the most unpopular GE subjects, and students are unlikely to attend PE courses. A total of 7.7 percent and 8.5 percent of the respondents classify advanced mathematics and English or foreign language, respectively, into the most unpopular category. Approximately 16 percent find

Table 4.1 Absence from university GE courses

	Estimated Overall Absence (%)	Self-Reported Absence (%)
Physical Education	2.6	2.3
Advanced Mathematics	7.7	6.9
English/Foreign Language	8.5	5.9
Computer Science	16.3	9.8
Military Theories	21.5	11.5
Political Education	69.8	52.7

Note: Respondents are allowed to choose up to three subjects, and thus the summation of the percentages in each column is not equal to 100 that students tend to be absent from computer science classes. A total of 21.5 percent of students believe that military theories is one of the subjects that their fellow students dislike the most. Up to 70 percent of the respondents identify political education as one of the most disliked subjects. Thus, political education is comparatively the least likable subject in universities.

This finding is further confirmed by self-reported absences recorded in the second column in Table 4.1. The self-reported absence does not appear to be as high as the estimation in the first column, which suggests that students are more reserved in reporting self-absence than disclosing the absence of their fellow classmates. This result is not necessarily because of political sensitivity but because of cognitive features. However, this outcome justifies the inclusion of the first survey question. Among the respondents, 2.3 percent report themselves likely to be absent from PE class, 6.9 percent from advanced mathematics, 5.9 percent from English or foreign languages, 9.8 percent from computer science, 11.5 percent from military theories, and 52.7 percent from political education. Thus, courses on political education are the least favored and most skipped by university students, which is parallel with Column 1. More than half of the respondents admit their high likelihood of being absent from political education classes.

The reasons for being absent are captured using an open-ended question. Table 4.2 lists the reasons given by those who have more absences in political education than other GE courses in universities. Among the total of 567 respondents who provided a reason, more than 40 percent note the boring classes and the lack of interest in the subject, and approximately 28 percent have conflicts with time and engage in other commitments. Seven percent believe that this course is useless in the future. Five percent point out that their absences will not affect their performance in any sense. Another 5 percent acknowledge that they dislike political doctrine. Eight students blame

Table 4.2 Reasons for absence from political education

	Observations	Percentage
No interest in boring classes	235	41.45
Time conflict	158	27.87
No use	39	6.88
No effect on class performance	29	5.11
Disliking doctrine	28	4.94
Too hard to understand	8	1.41
Redundancy	6	1.06
Others	64	11.29
Total	567	

the obscurity of teaching, and six contend that they have already learned these lessons in the past and teaching is redundant. Eleven percent provide different excuses for their absence, such as widespread absences in class, sickness or other personal reasons, distance of classrooms, or laziness in attending morning classes. A number of the respondents also emphasize that self-study is more efficient than attending classes, and they like to study at libraries by themselves instead of attending the class and listening to teachers.

Thus, the reasons of the respondents indicate that attending classes in political education is unlikely because of class performance, knowledge transfer, or peer pressure. Presence indicates compliance, and absence suggests resistance.

Explaining resistance to political indoctrination by Internet exposure

Instead of self-reported attitudes, this study adopts a behavioral measure of citizens' noncompliance with state propaganda. For operationalization, the dependent variable is measured dichotomously and coded as "1" if the respondent escapes most political teaching, and "0" otherwise. Key independent variables include the four measures of Internet exposure. Average daily Internet time and Internet age measure the intensity and history of Internet exposure. Exposure to online pluralistic horizontal communication captures the number of venues one is open to for communication with fellow netizens. Whether one reads online news, reads blog or microblog articles, goes to BBS forums, and searches through web encyclopedias, regarding public issues or affairs, are covered in the additive indicator. The variable ranges from 4 to 0; "4" is given if the respondent uses all four venues and "0" if he or she uses none. The variable of exposure to online vertical communication indicates the frequency of government web visits, which ranges from "4" for almost every day to "0" for never (for details, see Chapter 3).

The two variables of perceptions about the Chinese government utilizing the Internet to promote mutual understanding with citizens are included to see whether a positive image of the government in cyberspace can help reduce resistance. Average daily exposure time to traditional media instruments is also included for comparison (for detailed discussion, see Chapter 3). Some additional variables are controlled in the model, including CCP membership, monthly financial support from one's parents or other family members, parents' aggregate educational attainments and political backgrounds, and university ID. The demographic variables of age and gender are also controlled. Detailed summaries of all the variables are listed in the appendix.

Table 4.3 reports the logit regression analysis results, controlled for survey design effects and sampling probabilities (for details, see Chapter 3).

Table 4.3 Logit regression results controlled for survey design effects and sampling probabilities

DV = resistance to political education	B	Std. Err.
Internet Exposure		
Exposure to government websites	−0.212	0.144
Exposure horizontal communication	0.183	0.068**
Internet age	0.058	0.026*
Internet time	0.095	0.036**
Perceptions of Intermediary Internet between Government and Citizens		
Internet helping officials understand public opinion	0.019	0.064
Officials' blogs helping build an open government	−0.113	0.065
Exposure to Traditional Media		
Newspaper time	−0.190	0.174
TV time	−0.060	0.091
Radio time	−0.635	0.374
Control Variables		
CCP membership	−0.273	0.187
Economic background	0.115	0.145
Parents' educational attainments	−0.038	0.030
Parents' party memberships	−0.078	0.135
University ID (teaching = 1)	0.659	0.166***
Gender (male = 1)	0.267	0.165
Age	0.097	0.062
_cons	−2.204	1.317
Number of strata		2
Number of PSUs		318
Number of obs.		1173
Population size		1394666
Design df		316
F statistic (16, 301)		3.14
Prob > F		0.0001

Note: $*p \leq 0.05$; $**p \leq 0.01$; $***p \leq 0.001$

The data present some significant effects of Internet exposure on resistance to political teaching. When a person is exposed to more venues of online horizontal communication, spends more time on the Internet, and has a longer history with the Internet, he or she is more likely to be absent from political education classes. A one-score increase in the horizontal exposure raises the odds of resistance by approximately 20 percent (exp(0.183) = 1.2). For each additional daily hour spent on the Internet, the odds of resistance is elevated by roughly 10 percent (exp(0.095) = 1.1). For each additional Internet year, the odds increase by 6 percent (exp(0.058) = 1.06). Thus, the pluralistic nature of cyberspace counteracts top-down indoctrination.

On the contrary, exposure to vertical communication with the government through the Internet does not statistically decrease one's resistance to political teaching. Thus, although e-government establishment promotes regime support (as demonstrated in Chapter 3), it does not manage to ensure the compliance of young Chinese with political teaching. The significant correlation between e-government and regime support is indeed attributed to the government's efforts to open up the political process in cyberspace for consultation and to fight corruption, but not to reiterating political ideologies. Echoing the ruling ideologies is not sufficient to boost obedience and win the support of this group of educated young people.

The two perception variables do not pass the threshold of statistical significance. However, the variable on the role of the blogs of government officials in improving governance has an effect on a rather robust level (p = 0.08). Each unit increase in the agreement with the statement that the blogs or microblogs of government officials can help promote an open government decreases the odds of resistance by 11 percent (exp(−0.113) = 0.89). The positive image of the Chinese government in making efforts to build an open government may therefore lower resistance to political teaching among educated youth.

The findings of the extant literature do not agree on the role of traditional media in state propaganda in authoritarian regimes. Some studies generally confirm that traditional media function for political persuasion and indoctrination and promote political trust and regime legitimacy (Brady, 2006; Geddes and Zaller, 1989; Kennedy, 2009; Li, 2004; Shambaugh, 2007; Stockmann and Gallagher, 2011). However, other studies have suggested that traditional media exposure is negatively associated with trust in political institutions (Chen and Shi, 2001). Traditional media instruments in this study generally demonstrate no significant effect on political resistance, except for the radio at a borderline statistical significance level (p = 0.09). For each additional daily hour spent listening to the radio, the odds of resistance drop by 47 percent (exp(−0.635) = 0.53). However, 1,040 students, which comprise more than 81 percent of the total respondents, do not listen to the radio at all. Only 26 students listen to the radio for one or more daily hours on average. Hence, the radio is probably unable to generate a substantial and extensive influence on this group of educated youth. Overall, new media outperforms old ones in shaping the political behavior of the educated young Chinese today.

Another interesting finding is the effect of university ID. According to statistically and substantively significant results, students from the normal teaching university are more likely to escape political education than their counterparts in another regular comprehensive university. Although intense institutional control and ethics teaching may produce a group of students that is supportive of the regime and hesitant to embrace democratic values (as indicated in Chapter 3), the institutional setup is insufficient to keep these students in a classroom with boring political teaching.

Other variables do not significantly influence the dependent variable. A CCP member may resist political indoctrination in a university as much as a non-member. Neither family economic conditions nor parents' political and socioeconomic backgrounds exert any explanatory power to political resistance. The disobedience of students cannot be explained by demographic features.

Conclusion

The statistical results in this chapter indicate a significant relationship between Internet exposure and resistance to political indoctrination. Multiple indicators of Internet exposure impose a statistically and substantively significant effect on one's likelihood to resist the teaching of ruling ideologies in universities. The results imply a profound crisis of the ruling ideologies among educated young Chinese. The traditional propaganda instruments, such as school and the old media, are no longer functioning as expected by the party state on this digital generation. Intense institutional control and substantial ethics teaching do not sufficiently keep students in the classroom of political education. On the contrary, tight regulations may drive them to defy the government's attempt to control their thinking. E-government can help maintain regime support, but does not systematically reduce one's disobedience in political education. The political propaganda system in China is declining. The Chinese government must depend on other means to legitimize the regime. Nationalism works as an alternative to enhancing national cohesion and pride.

Note

1 The scope of state propaganda oversight includes "newspaper offices, radio stations, television stations, publishing houses, magazines, and other news and media departments; universities, middle schools, primary schools, and other vocational education, specialized education, cadre training, and other educational organs . . ." Zhongguo Gongchandang jianshe dazidian 1921–1991 (An Encyclopedia on the Building of the CCP), quoted by Shambaugh (2007).

References

Balkin, Jack M. 2004. Digital Speech and Democratic Culture: A Theory of Freedom of Expression for the Information Society. *New York University Law Review*, 79, 1–5.

Baum, Richard. 2008. Political Implications of China's Information Revolution: The Media, The Minders, and Their Message. In *China's Changing Political Landscape: Prospects for Democracy*, edited by Cheng Li, pp. 161–184. Washington, DC: Brookings.

Benkler, Yochai. 2006. *The Wealth of Networks: How Social Production Transforms Markets and Freedom*. New Haven, CT: Yale University Press.

Brady, Anne-Marie. 2006. Guiding Hand: The Role of the CCP Central Propaganda Department in the Current Era. *Westminster Papers in Communication and Culture*, 3(1), 58–77.

Chen, Xueyi, and Tianjian Shi. 2001. Media Effects on Political Confidence and Trust in the PRC in the Post-Tiananmen Period. *East Asia: An International Quarterly*, 19(3), 84–118.

Dahlgren, Peter. 2000. The Internet and the Democratization of Civic Culture. *Political Communication*, 17, 335–340.

The Economist. December 13, 2014. Propaganda 2.0. Retrieved from www.economist. com/news/china/21636090-once-caught-back-foot-social-media-communist-party-has-upgraded-its-propaganda.

Esarey, Ashley and Xiao Qiang. 2011. Digital Communication and Political Change in China. *International Journal of Communication*, 5, 298–319.

Fairbrother, Gregory P. 2003. *Toward Critical Patriotism: Student Resistance to Political Education in Hong Kong and China*. Hong Kong: The University of Hong Kong Press.

Fairbrother, Gregory P. 2004. Patriotic Education in a Chinese Middle School. In *Citizenship Education in Asia and the Pacific: Concepts and Issues*, edited by W. O. Lee, D. L. Grossman, K. J. Kennedy, and G. P. Fairbrother, pp. 157–174. Dordrecht, Netherlands: Kluwer Academic Publishers.

Fairbrother, Gregory. 2008. Rethinking Hegemony and Resistance to Political Education in Mainland China and Hong Kong. *Comparative Education Review*, 52(3), 381–412.

Geddes Barbara and John Zaller. 1989. Sources of Support for Authoritarian Regimes. *American Journal of Political Science*, 33(2), 319–347.

Kalathil, Shanthi. 2002. Chinese Media and the Information Revolution. *Harvard Asia Quarterly*, Winter. Retrieved from www.ceip.org/files/publications/kalathil_harvardasia.asp.

Kalathil, Shanthi and Taylor C. Boas. 2003. *Open Networks, Closed Regimes: The Impact of the Internet on Authoritarian Rule*. Washington, DC: Carnegie Endowment for International Peace.

Kennedy John J. 2009. Maintaining Popular Support for the Chinese Communist Party: The Influence of Education and the State-Controlled Media. *Political Studies*, 57, 517–536.

Lei, Ya-Wen. 2011. The Political Consequences of the Rise of the Internet: Political Beliefs and Practices of Chinese Netizens. *Political Communication*, 28(3), 291–322.

Li, Lianjiang. 2004. Political Trust in Rural China. *Modern China*, 30(2), 228–258.

MacKinnon, Rebecca. 2007. Flatter World and Thicker Walls? Blogs, Censorship and Civic Discourse in China. *Public Choice*, 134(1–2), 31–46.

MacKinnon, Rebecca. 2011. China's "Networked Authoritarianism". *Journal of Democracy*, 22(2), 32–46.

Pang, Haishao. 2010. University General Education Courses in China: Implications, Current Status and Prospects. *University General Education Bulletin*, 6, 91–112.

Propaganda Department of the Chinese Communist Party Central Committee and the Ministry of Education. 2005. *Advice on Further Strengthening and Improving the Courses on Thoughts and Political Theories in Higher Education* ([2005] No. 5).

Rosen, Stanley. 1993. The Effects of Post-4 June Re-education Campaign on Chinese Students. *The China Quarterly*, 134, 310–334.

Scott, James C. 1985. *Weapons of the Weak: Everyday Forms of Peasant Resistance.* New Haven, CT: Yale University Press.

Shambaugh, David. 2007. China's Propaganda System: Institutions, Processes and Efficacy. *The China Journal*, 57, 25–58.

Stockmann, Daniela. 2013. *Media Commercialization and Authoritarian Rule in China.* New York: Cambridge University Press.

Stockmann, Daniela and Mary E. Gallagher. 2011. Remote Control: How the Media Sustains Authoritarian Rule in China. *Comparative Political Studies*, 44(4), 436–467.

Sullivan, Jonathan. 2012. A Tale of Two Microblogs in China. *Media, Culture & Society*, 34(6), 773–783.

Tang, Lijun and Helen Sampson. 2012. The Interaction Between Mass Media and the Internet in Non-Democratic States: The Case of China. *Media, Culture & Society*, 34(4), 457–471.

Tang, Lijun and Peidong Yang. 2011. Symbolic Power and the Internet: The Power of a "Horse". *Media, Culture & Society*, 33(5), 675–691.

Tang, Min and Narison Huhe. 2014. Alternative Framing: The Effect of the Internet on Political Support in Authoritarian China. *International Political Science Review*, 35(5), 559–576.

Taubman, Geoffrey. 1998. A Not-So World Wide Web: The Internet, China, and the Challenges to Nondemocratic Rule. *Political Communication*, 15(2), 255–272.

Tong, Yanqi and Shaohua Lei. 2013. War of Position and Microblogging in China. *Journal of Contemporary China*, 22(80), 292–311.

Yang, Guobin. 2003. The Internet and Civil Society in China: A Preliminary Assessment. *Journal of Contemporary China*, 12(36), 453–475.

Yang, Guobin. 2009a. *The Power of the Internet in China: Citizen Activism Online.* New York: Columbia University Press.

Yang, Guobin. 2009b. Online Activism. *Journal of Democracy*, 20(3), 33–36.

Zheng, Yongnian. 2008. *Technological Empowerment: The Internet, State and Society in China.* Stanford, CA: Stanford University Press.

Zhou, Xiang. 2009. The Political Blogosphere in China: A Content Analysis of the Blogs regarding the Dismissal of Shanghai Leader Chen Liangyu. *New Media and Society*, 11(6), 1003–1022.

5 Internet exposure and nationalism

Introduction

Nationalism among Chinese has been recently fueled by the ruling of The Hague on the South China Sea on July 12, 2016. The maritime rights and territorial sovereignty previously claimed by the Chinese government over the region was rejected by the verdict. The Chinese state media, Xinhua News Agency, immediately responded and rejected the verdict as "ill founded" and "naturally null and void" (The New York Times, August 13, 2016; Phillips, Holmes, and Bowcott, 2016). At the grassroots level, a nationalist sentiment assisted by new social media instruments has rapidly dominated public discourse.

The Chinese government has recently taken a fairly aggressive stand in the South China Sea disputes. Nevertheless, Chinese leaders stay alert toward popular nationalism that may go out of control and jeopardize foreign relations and, more importantly, challenge the rule of the party state (The Economist, July 23, 2016; Gries, 2005; Shen and Westcott, July 21, 2016;). On July 15, 2016, the overseas edition of *People's Daily* continued to report in detail the anger and criticism of netizens regarding the verdict in a rather positive tone (Chai, July 15, 2016). However, articles published on the official news agency Xinhua and *People's Daily* both emphasized that patriotism should stay rational and criticized the collective actions as "disruptive" right after the simultaneous occurrence of protests and boycotts targeting KFC, iPhone, and Filipino fruit in multiple Chinese cities (Shen and Westcott, July 21, 2016; O, July 21, 2016).

This instance demonstrates both the complicated nature of nationalism and the mixed feelings of the state toward it. On one hand, nationalism helps maintain the legitimacy of the authoritarian regime. Patriotic education and indoctrination remain the objectives of state media and school education. As a result, Chinese people, especially young students, possess a strong sense of nationalism (Bregnbæk, 2016). On the other hand, the party state has become increasingly incapable of controlling nationalism at the grassroots level in China (Gries, 2005). With the assistance of newly developed information and communications technologies, "popular nationalists in China are increasingly able to act independently of the state" (Gries, 2005, p. 245). Empirical evidence suggests that popular nationalism clearly differentiates the party and the nation, and popular national pride may not be necessarily transformed to support for the party state (Gries, 2004 and 2005; Liu, 2011; Woods and Dickson, 2016; Wu, 2007). This double-edged popular sentiment sometimes pressures the state, and failing to address the expectations of popular nationalists may invite criticism, which in turn weakens the legitimacy of the Chinese Communist Party (CCP)'s rule. Given the domestic political conditions, political leaders may be forced to compromise in order to retain the consent of the Chinese people (Gries, 2005; Weiss, 2014).

Understanding nationalism in China

Chinese nationalism did not emerge until China was forcefully opened up by foreign colonial powers in the mid-19th century (Pye, 1990; Zhao, 2004; Zheng, 1999; Liu, 2011). Open-minded Chinese intellectuals began to realize that China was not any more the center of civilization, but only one of the nations in the world that had already lagged behind the path of development and modernization (Chang, 1987; Harrison, 2000; Liu, 2011). This group of intellectuals, including Dr. Sun Yat-sen, proposed nationalism as an ideology to fight foreign imperialism and modernize China by emphasizing an identity derived from the concept of "China" (Tok, 2010). As a result of disappointment at the increasingly corrupt and weak Qing government and accumulated humiliations from the frequent defeats by foreign imperialism, the nationalist reaction mainly emphasized a strong nation free from being victimized by foreign imperialism (Liu, 2011; Zhao, 2004; Zheng, 1999).

Chinese nationalism refers to two different aspects. First, feelings and attitudes derived from a victim mentality focus on antagonism and competition between China and other nations in an "us" versus "them" framework and emphasize strategies that prevent China from being victimized by superpowers. Second, national pride denotes a strong attachment (and positive sentiment) to national identity, concentrates on an in-group relationship, and is likely derived from the achievements of the nation (cultural, economic, historical, etc.) (Gries et al., 2011; Woods and Dickson, 2016; Zhang and Stening, 2010).

People attribute nationalism to different sources. Although a few believe that nationalism comes from a primordial identity, that is, national identity and nationalist sentiments are something one is born with rather than acquired and "inherently irrational" and transcend individual interests (Hardin, 1995, p. 14; Zhao, 2004; Liu, 2011), the later development of nationalism in China featured a process of social reconstruction, that is, nationalism is constructed through socialization via mass media or other instruments (Anderson, 1991; Liu, 2011). The main content of nationalism under Mao's rule was changed to an indoctrinated idea of self-reliance that attempted to overtake imperialist enemies. Afterward, nationalism was reconstructed from the top down in the name of patriotism as an alternative to gradually declining Marxism and Communism to maintain the legitimacy of the rule of the party state, especially after the 1989 Tiananmen Square Movement (Gries, 2005; Huang and Lee, 2003; Liu, 2011; Xu, 2001; Zhao, 2004; Zheng, 1999).

State-led patriotic education campaigns were intensively carried out on mass media and in school since the 1990s to ensure the loyalty of the Chinese population to the party state and reverse its declining legitimacy (Huang and Lee, 2003; Zhao, 1998). In particular, the official recount of the history of humiliations before 1949 was repeatedly instilled in the Chinese education system (Bregnbæk, 2016; Tok, 2010). Students are taught to love both their country and the party because the new nation they love would not have existed if not for the party (Bregnbæk, 2016). The editorial of *Qiushi*, the theory journal of the Central Party Committee, clearly asserted in 1990 that patriotism meant loving socialist China under the rule of the CCP, and one could not and should not differentiate motherland from socialism, which set the tone of the official version of patriotism today (Huang and Lee, 2003).

The signature concept of the "China Dream" by Chinese president Xi Jinping was officially inaugurated in late 2012 and aimed to achieve "the great rejuvenation of the Chinese nation" (Callahan, 2013). Although no official interpretation exists, the concept must include continuous economic development that has long been used to sustain national pride, legitimize authoritarianism, and mobilize regime support in the official discourse (Tok, 2010). The China Dream concept of Xi also implicitly echoes the 2010 book of Prof. Liu Mingfu titled *China Dream: Great Power Thinking and Strategies Posture in the Post-American Era* (Callahan, 2013; Terhalle, 2015). As a professor at the National Defense University of China and a senior colonel of the People's Liberation Army, Liu strongly urges in his book that economic reform has been emphasized too much, and China should now shift her attention to military development and acquire a rapid military rise to defend her economic achievement and counterbalance the U.S. power (Callahan, 2013; Terhalle, 2015).

Since the late 1990s, especially after the inauguration of the fourth-generation leadership of China in 2002, official military spending has rapidly increased. Between 2000 and 2016, the official military spending has mostly maintained an annual double-digit increase (data from GlobalSecurity. org, 2016, www.globalsecurity.org/military/world/china/budget.htm). In response to the "China threat" argument derived from the international uncertainties regarding the continuously rising military power of China, the Chinese official discourse frequently emphasizes that China is concerned with a "peaceful rise." Military uprising is a crucial but tacit component of the China Dream. The military achievement of China has not been acclaimed as often as her economic accomplishment. Nevertheless, the public can discern the rising military power of China from certain events, such as the military parade on National Day. Military uprising comprises another component of the "China Dream" and contributes to official patriotism, apart from economic prosperity.

By contrast, popular nationalism, a bottom-up sentiment, is derived from a victim mentality and is essentially reactive to external provocations and lacks a solid ideological ground (Hyun et al., 2014; Shen and Breslin, 2010; Wu, 2007; Zhao, 1998 and 2005). Popular nationalism is reinforced through the horizontal dialog among the public, especially fueled by a few opinion leaders who also ventilate their nationalist emotions and may deviate from state-led patriotic education (Gries, 2005; Hyun et al., 2014; Liu, 2010; Woods and Dickson, 2016; Wu, 2007; Zhao, 2005). This distinction bears a profound implication; although both official and popular nationalisms are innately anti-Western, comprise a feeling of pride in a type of national glory, and hope for China to become a strong nation in the future, the two can diverge or even conflict if the understanding of the public of what has happened and how to deal with it differs from the interpretation of the government. For instance, a few posts on the Strong Nation Forum (*qiang-guo luntan*, www.qglt.com/bbs/start), which is an online forum affiliated with *People's Daily*, squarely challenged the tone of the state when the state media attempted to constrain the anti-Japan protest and called for harmony in 2005 (Liu, 2010). This chapter in particular investigates how media exposure, especially Internet exposure, affects the two potentially contesting nationalisms.

Internet exposure and nationalism

Previous literature suggests that exposure to state-controlled traditional media helps indoctrinate official nationalism into citizens' minds (Guo et al., 2007; Huang and Lee, 2003; Hyun et al., 2014; Zhao, 1998). A few studies focus on nationalism online in China (Jiang, 2012; Liu, 2010; Reilly, 2010; Shen and Breslin, 2010; Wu, 2007). Popular nationalism can be bred and intensified via various Internet platforms (e.g., blogs, BBS forums, and other social networking instruments). Nationalists can discuss possible offline strategies and overcome the coordination problem via horizontal communication online (Jiang, 2012; Liu, 2010). However, the effect of Internet exposure on nationalism has not been comprehensively studied. The establishment of e-government may deliver the same type of political teaching as on state-owned mass media and in school, attempting to indoctrinate the ruling ideology from the top down. But previous chapters suggest that although e-government improves regime support, it cannot prevent university students from resisting political teaching. By contrast, exposure to the interactions of netizens who sometimes become critical of the state tone may end up formulating a popular nationalist discourse from the bottom up as an alternative to the official one (Gries, 2004; Liu, 2010; Woods and Dickson, 2016; Wu, 2007). Statistical analysis is conducted as follows to figure out the influences of Internet exposure in this aspect.

Measures of nationalism

A list of observed indicators capturing nationalism from various perspectives is incorporated in this study. These perspectives include pride in socialist China, confidence in the future economic achievement of China, belief that China should become the top military superpower in the world, online petitions against a foreign country, and online celebrations on traditional national festivals or important national events in China.

Pride in socialism

The agreement level of university students with the statement "I feel proud of our socialist China" on a 5-point Likert scale with "1" indicating strongly disagreeing and "5" strongly agreeing specifies official patriotism. More than three-quarters of the sample students agree or strongly agree with this statement. Another 17 percent disagree or strongly disagree with the statement (mini-chart 1 in Figure 5.1).

Confidence in China's economy

Another source of national pride comes from the grand economic success of China. Pride and confidence derived from China's economic miracle have become a reliable and stable ground for nationalism. The level of agreement with the statement "I am fully confident that China will become an economic superpower in the 21st century" is recorded on the same 5-point Likert scale. The mini-chart 2 in Figure 5.1 demonstrates that approximately three-quarters of the students agree or strongly agree with this view. By contrast, more than one-fifth of the sample students disagree.

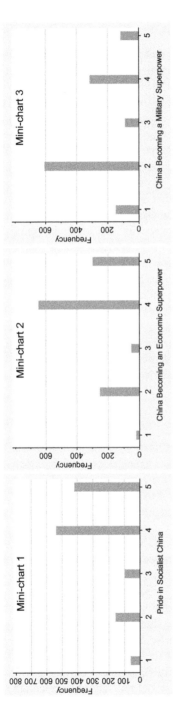

Figure 5.1 Official patriotism of university students

Note: Mini-chart 1 is adapted from mini-chart 2 in Figure 3.2.

Survey Questions:

Do you strongly agree, agree, stay neutral, disagree, or strongly disagree with the following statements?

Mini-chart 1: I feel proud of our socialist China.

Mini-chart 2: I am fully confident that China will become an economic superpower in the 21st century.

Mini-chart 3: Prof. Liu Mingfu pointed out in his book *China Dream* that China should build the strongest military force in the world and compete with the United States. In his book, Prof. Liu emphasized that "becoming the top military superpower in the world is the goal of China for the 21st century." Do you strongly agree, agree, stay neutral, disagree, or strongly disagree with his view?

Belief in China's military capacity

The idea of simultaneously building an economically wealthy and militarily powerful state (*fu guo qiang bing*) appeared in ancient Chinese works as early as 2,000 years ago (Guan and Rickett, 1965). Economic and military powers have all along been regarded as the two capacities that can jointly strengthen a nation. Belief in China's military capacity is also included to capture its contribution to nationalism. A survey question asks the extent to which the subject agrees with Prof. Liu's idea that China should emulate the United States and become the top military superpower in the world in the 21st century on the same 5-point Likert scale. According to mini-chart 3 in Figure 5.1, majority of the students disagree with this view and do not acknowledge that China should become a military superpower to defend herself. Specifically, more than one-tenth strongly disagree with this idea, and approximately 48 percent disagree. Only one-third of the students strongly agree or agree with this assertion. Thus, in contrast with the perception regarding China's economy, the educated youth in China hesitate to accept an intense military contestation, which indicates considerable military expenditure. On one hand, the relatively low degree of agreement in this case is probably because China's military accomplishment has not been extensively incorporated in national pride upon the taciturnity of the Chinese government. On the other hand, this relatively low level of agreement may be attributed to the adopted antimilitarism of the largely post-materialist–educated youth.

Online nationalist actions

Online nationalism is also captured in this set of measures. Rather than idiosyncratic verbal expressions, this chapter documents nationalist cyberactivism. Online collective actions are more efficient and less costly than those on the streets are. Two types of nationalist activism are documented in the survey as manifestations of popular nationalism, including petitions against a foreign country/a boycott against a foreign enterprise and celebrations for a Chinese traditional festival/important national event. The indicators are coded as "2" if the subject is not only a participant but also an organizer of such a collective action, "1" if the subject is only a participant, and "0" otherwise. The survey was conducted in a "normal" phase in international relations when online nationalism did not dominate the cyberspace. Table 5.1 illustrates that six students have initiated an online petition against a foreign country or enterprise. Another 73 students have participated in such an action. Altogether, more than 6 percent of the students have participated in nationalist petitions online. Fourteen university students in the sample have initiated an online sign-up to celebrate national

Table 5.1 Nationalist collective actions in cyberspace

	Online Celebration on a Traditional Festival or National Event		Online Petition against a Foreign Country or Enterprise	
	Freq.	*Percent*	*Freq.*	*Percent*
Nonparticipation (0)	1,043	81.48	1,201	93.83
Participant (1)	223	17.42	73	5.7
Organizer (2)	14	1.09	6	0.47
Total	1,280	100	1,280	100

glory. Another 223 have participated. Altogether, approximately 19 percent of the sample have shown their love for China in this manner.

Principal component analysis

A principal component analysis (PCA) based on the polychoric correlation through a maximum likelihood procedure is conducted to construct the latent variables of official patriotism and popular nationalism. As mentioned in Chapter 3, this procedure is based on the assumption that latent constructs are continuous and normally distributed and the observed variables are ordinal measures (Drasgow, 1988; Kolenikov and Angeles, 2009). The two latent constructs are identified from the results of nonorthogonal (oblimin) rotation of the PCA according to the Kaiser criterion ($\rho = 0.62$), with their eigenvalues at 1.78 and 1.30 (Kaiser, 1960). Rotation is used for the optimization of loadings, and nonorthogonal rotation allows a correlation between the two dimensions.

Table 5.2 demonstrates the loadings of the preceding five items on these two dimensions. The items of pride in socialism and confidence in the economic capacity of China acquire the greatest loadings (>0.6) on the first dimension, followed by the view that China should become the top military superpower (roughly 0.4). The two remaining items, which are petition against a foreign country/enterprise and celebration of a national festival/event, only contribute minimally to this dimension. Thus, the first dimension represents top-down indoctrinated official patriotism. The first two items provide the most contributions because they are explicitly emphasized in political education and official discourse. However, the message regarding military achievement is likely implicitly derived to the public and thus contributes less than the first two items. The last two items do not contribute to the first dimension.

By contrast, the last two items contribute the greatest loadings to the second dimension (both roughly 0.7), to which the first three items contribute

Table 5.2 Principal component analysis loadings (oblimin rotation)

Items	Official Patriotism	Popular Nationalism
I feel proud of our socialist China	0.6385	−0.0699
I am fully confident that China will become an economic superpower in the 21st century	0.6526	0.0335
China should build the strongest military force in the world and compete with the United States.	0.4089	0.128
Protest against a foreign country or a foreign enterprise	−0.0023	0.7126
Celebration of a Chinese traditional festival or an important national event	0.0000	0.686
Eigenvalues	1.782	1.29722
% of common variance	0.3564	0.2594
Cumulative % of common variance (ρ) = 0.6158		

much smaller loadings. Pride in socialism and confidence in China's economy do not contribute to the second factor significantly. Belief in China's military capacity presents a comparatively greater loading than the two; nevertheless, it remains incomparable to the last two items. The second dimension represents bottom-up popular nationalism collectively expressed in cyberspace. Nationalist protests on the streets are not included in this study because they are sensitive and costly actions, and probably even rare events. Online nationalism is a sufficient and inclusive indicator of expressed popular nationalism, especially for the Internet-savvy group of subjects. The aggregate measures of the two dimensions, which include latent dependent variables, official patriotism score, and popular nationalism score, are computed based on the PCA results.

Explaining official patriotism and popular nationalism

As in the previous chapters, the same set of independent variables is covered in this statistical analysis. Multiple measures of Internet exposure, perceptions regarding the role of the Internet in the communication between the government and netizens, and exposure to traditional media are all captured in the regressions in this chapter. Control variables, such as political and socioeconomic backgrounds, educational and political backgrounds of parents, and demographic characteristics, are also covered in the analysis (for details, see Chapter 3). Ordinary least squares (OLS) regression results controlling for survey effects and sampling probabilities are reported in Table 5.3.

Table 5.3 OLS regression results controlled for survey design effects and sampling probabilities

	Model 1: DV=Official Patriotism		Model 2: DV=Popular Nationalism	
	B	Std. Err.	B	Std. Err.
Internet Exposure				
Exposure to Government Websites	0.152	0.091	0.065	0.027*
Exposure Horizontal communication	−0.055	0.041	0.048	0.012***
Internet age	−0.013	0.017	0.004	0.005
Internet time	−0.037	0.031	0.004	0.006
Perceptions of Intermediary Internet between Government and Citizens				
Internet helping officials understand public opinion	0.091	0.044*	−0.018	0.013
Officials' blogs helping build an open government	0.173	0.049***	0.006	0.013
Exposure to Traditional Media				
Newspaper time	0.100	0.096	0.034	0.032
TV time	0.076	0.056	−0.019	0.014
Radio time	0.118	0.218	−0.003	0.044
Control Variables				
CCP membership	0.254	0.151	−0.063	0.042
Economic background	0.011	0.099	0.059	0.032
Parents' educational attainments	−0.040	0.019*	−0.003	0.005
Parents' party memberships	0.077	0.084	−0.028	0.026
University ID (teaching=1)	0.178	0.093	−0.016	0.027
Gender (male=1)	0.269	0.108*	0.076	0.030*
Age	−0.082	0.039*	−0.021	0.011
_cons	6.886	0.834***	0.389	0.248
Number of strata	2		2	
Number of PSUs	318		318	
Number of obs.	1164		1164	
Population size	1385662		1385662	
Design df	316		316	
F(16, 301) statistic	4.69		2.97	
Prob > F	0.0000		0.0001	
R-squared	0.0826		0.0617	

Note: *$p \leq 0.05$; **$p \leq 0.01$; ***$p \leq 0.001$

Analysis and results

Table 5.3 presents the regression results of the two models. Model 1 covers the analysis results of official patriotism, and Model 2 nationalist cyberactivism. The statistical results of the two models illustrate distinctive stories. Internet exposure is correlated to both official patriotism and popular nationalism, but in different ways. Model 1 shows that none of the Internet exposure measures are able to exert a statistically significant influence on official patriotism. Exposure to e-government has a relationship with the dependent variable at a borderline significance level (p = 0.094). For each level increase in the frequency of government web visits, the patriotism score increases by 0.15, holding other factors constant.

As discussed in Chapter 3, causality between exposure to e-government and patriotism is difficult to confirm. On one hand, visiting e-government may promote patriotism if online political teaching entrenched in the government websites is functioning. On the other hand, the process may be endogenous; patriotic people may simply tend to visit government websites in the same way as they read state-controlled newspapers or watch state-owned China Central Television (CCTV), which makes them even more patriotic. As in the previous chapters, two variables perceiving the role of the Internet in political communication are included in the regression models.

The effect of Internet exposure on official patriotism is also embedded in the two perception variables. Portraying the Internet as a medium to enhance the communication between government and netizens is positively associated with official patriotism. These two independent variables indirectly measure one's evaluations of the Internet use of the Chinese government. Those who perceive that the Chinese government utilizes the Internet in promoting government–citizen communication tend to be patriotic. Specifically, one level increase in the agreement with the statement that the Internet assists officials to understand public opinion increases the official patriotism score by 0.09, and that with the statement that blogs of government officials help build an open government increases official patriotism by 0.17. Hence, even though actual exposure to vertical communication may not cause patriotism, the Chinese government can manage to boost patriotism among netizens by engineering an image of a responsive government on the Internet.

By contrast, Model 2 shows that exposure to both vertical and horizontal communications exerts a positive effect on popular nationalism at a statistically significant level. For each level increase in the frequency of government web visits, the score of popular nationalism increases by approximately 0.07; for each additional online venue used for horizontal communication, popular nationalism increases by 0.05. Thus, those who are exposed to cyberpolitics generally tend to express their nationalism online. The general indicators of Internet exposure, Internet time, and Internet age exert no effect, nor do the perception variables.

Exposure to old media imposes no effect on official patriotism or on popular nationalism, because political indoctrination engaged in by state-owned traditional media is largely redundant to those under intensive political education in school. The CCP membership exerts no influence on popular nationalism. A party member is not necessarily more popularly nationalist than a nonmember is. However, membership is relatively significantly correlated to patriotism (p = 0.095). A party member is, on average, 0.25 more patriotic than a nonmember is. The economic background of a person affects popular nationalism, but not official patriotism, with regard to statistics. For a mean value increase in financial aid from the family, that is, roughly 778 RMB, the score of popular nationalism increases by 0.06 (p = 0.065). Data also show that students with highly educated parents tend to be systematically less patriotic than those with less educated parents, probably because educated parents have taught their children to be critical of political persuasion. But substantively it does not make a big contribution. Each level increase in parents' educational attainments leads to a 0.04 reduction in one's patriotism score. Parents' CCP memberships exert no systematic influence on patriotism. Parents' socioeconomic and political backgrounds impose no effect on popular nationalism, either.

The coefficient of university ID appears very close to the 0.05 statistical significance threshold (p = 0.058), even though it does not pass it in Model 1. Students from a normal teaching university are generally 0.178 more patriotic than their counterparts from a comprehensive university, holding other factors constant. However, they are not systematically different from one another in terms of popular nationalism. The findings that party members and those from normal teaching universities tend to express greater patriotism than others probably imply that institutional constraints can sustain their loyalty to the state, at least in expression, although these factors are incapable of reducing resistance to political teaching, as discussed in Chapter 4.

The results also demonstrate that male and younger students tend to be more patriotic than female and older students are. A male student, all else being equal, is on average 0.27 more patriotic than a female student is. For each additional year of age, the score of official patriotism decreases by 0.08. The variable of gender also statistically significantly explains popular nationalism. A male student is approximately 0.08 more popularly nationalist than a female student, other factors being equal. Age is also negatively associated with popular nationalism, only at a less statistical significance level (p = 0.065). Each year of age increase, on average, yields a 0.02 decrease in popular nationalism.

Conclusion

Although the Internet is not a good place for political propaganda, it can be used to showcase the effort of the government to build a responsive and open system and assist the government in winning back the loyalty of citizens and enhancing their national pride. Institutional features, such as Communist Party membership and the institutional constraints in normal teaching universities in China, continue to possess binding power in expressed official patriotism among university students. These factors nevertheless impose no effect on popular nationalism. Socioeconomic factors, such as family economic background and parents' educational achievements, as well as demographic features, explain different types of nationalism of university students. University students with educated parents express less patriotism than those with low-educated parents. Those from relatively wealthy families tend to engage in cyberactivism to express popular nationalism (albeit at a less statistically significant level than 0.05). Younger male students tend to be more nationalist than older female ones.

References

Anderson, Benedict. 1991. *Imagined Communities: Reflections on the Origin and Spread of Nationalism*, Revised Edition. New York: Verso.

Bregnbæk, Susanne. 2016. *Fragile Elite: The Dilemmas of China's Top University Students*. Palo Alto, CA: Stanford University Press.

Callahan, William A. 2013. *China Dreams: 20 Visions of the Future*. Oxford: Oxford University Press.

Chai, Yifei (柴逸扉). July 15, 2016. Not Accepted, Not Acknowledged: Netizens Devotedly Discussed the Recent Ruling of The Hague on the South China Sea (不接受, 不承认 – 网友热议"南海仲裁案"), *People's Daily, overseas edition*. Retrieved from http://paper.people.com.cn/rmrbhwb/html/2016-07/15/content_1695542.htm.

Chang, Hao. 1987. *Chinese Intellectuals in Crisis: Search for Order and Meaning, 1890–1911*. Berkeley: University of California Press.

Drasgow, Fritz. 1988. Polychoric and Polyserial Correlations. In *Encyclopedia of Statistical Sciences*, Vol. 7, edited by L. Kotz and N. L. Johnson, pp. 69–74. New York: Wiley.

The Economist. July 23, 2016. My Nationalism, and Don't You Forget It. Retrieved from www.economist.com/news/china/21702527-xi-jinping-tries-contain-public-fury-over-south-china-sea-my-nationalism-and-dont-you.

GlobalSecurity.org. 2016. *China's Defense Budget*. Retrieved from www.globalsecurity.org/military/world/china/budget.htm.

Gries, P. H. 2004. *China's New Nationalism: Pride, Politics, and Diplomacy*. Berkeley: University of California Press.

Gries, P. H. September 2005. Chinese Nationalism: Challenging the State? *Current History*, 104, 251–256.

Gries, P. H., Qingmin Zhang, H. Michael Crowson, and Huajian Cai. 2011. Patriotism, Nationalism and China's US Policy: Structures and Consequences of Chinese National Identity. *The China Quarterly*, 205, 1–17.

Guan, Z. and W. A. Rickett. 1965. *Guanzi*. Hong Kong: Hong Kong University Press.

Guo, Z., W. H. Cheong, and H. Chen. 2007. Nationalism as Public Imagination: The Media's Routine Contribution to Latent and Manifest Nationalism in China. *The International Communication Gazette*, 69, 467–480.

Hardin, Russell. 1995. *One for All: The Logic of Group Conflict*. Princeton: Princeton University Press.

Harrison, Henrietta. 2000. Newspapers and Nationalism in Rural China 1890–1929. *Past & Present*, 166, 181–204.

Huang, Y. and C. Lee. 2003. Peddling Party Ideology for a Profit: Media and the Rise of Chinese Nationalism in the 1990s. In *Political Communications in Greater China: The Construction and Reflection of Identity*, edited by G. D. Rawnsley and M. T. Rawnsley, pp. 41–61. London: Routledge Curzon.

Hyun, K., J. Kim, and S. Sun. 2014. News Use, Nationalism, and Internet Use Motivations as Predictors of Anti-Japanese Political Actions in China. *Asian Journal of Communication*, 24, 589–604.

Jiang, Ying. 2012. *Cyber-Nationalism in China: Challenging Western Media Portrayals of Internet Censorship in China*. Adelaide: University of Adelaide Press.

Kaiser, H. F. 1960. The Application of Electronic Computers to Factor Analysis. *Educational and Psychological Measurement*, 20, 141–151.

Kolenikov, Stanislav and Gustavo Angeles. 2009. Socioeconomic Status Measurement with Discrete Proxy Variables: Is Principal Component Analysis a Reliable Answer? *The Review of Income and Wealth*, 55(1), 128–165.

Liu, Fengshu. 2011. *Urban Youth in China: Modernity, the Internet and the Self*. New York: Routledge.

Liu, Shih-Diing. 2010. Networking Anti-Japanese Protests. In *Online Chinese Nationalism and China's Bilateral Relations*, edited by Simon Shen and Shaun Breslin. London: Lexington Books, pp. 73–90.

The New York Times. August 13, 2016. China's Defiance in the South China Sea. Editorial. Retrieved from www.nytimes.com/2016/08/14/opinion/sunday/chinas-defiance-in-the-south-china-sea.html?_r=0.

O, Gwangjin (吴光镇). July 21, 2016. Collective Actions Against KFC Appeared in China and Official Media Emphasizes Rational Patriotism (中国出现抵制KFC 运动 官媒强调"理性爱国"). *Chinese News Chosun Biz*. Retrieved from http://cnnews.chosun.com/client/news/viw.asp?cate=C01&mcate=M1002&nNewsNumb=20160745470&nidx=45471.

Phillips, Tom, Oliver Holmes, and Owen Bowcott. July 12, 2016. Beijing Rejects Tribunal's Ruling in South China Sea Case. *The Guardian*. Retrieved from www.theguardian.com/world/2016/jul/12/philippines-wins-south-china-sea-case-against-china.

Pye, Lucian. 1990. China: Erratic State, Frustrated Society. *Foreign Affairs*, 69(4), 56–74.

Reilly, James. 2010. China's Online Nationalism Toward Japan. In *Online Chinese Nationalism and China's Bilateral Relations*, edited by Simon Shen and Shaun Breslin. London: Lexington Books, pp. 45–72.

Shen, Lu and Ben Westcott. July 21, 2016. South China Sea: Beijing Calls KFC, Apple Protests "Irrational". *CNN News*. Retrieved from http://edition.cnn.com/2016/07/20/asia/china-nationalism-south-china-sea-ruling/.

Shen, Simon and Shaun Breslin (eds.). 2010. *Online Chinese Nationalism and China's Bilateral Relations*. London: Lexington Books.

Terhalle, M. 2015. *The Transition of Global Order: Legitimacy and Contestation*. New York: Springer.

Tok, Sow Keat. 2010. Nationalism-On-Demand? When Chinese Sovereignty Goes Online. In *Online Chinese Nationalism and China's Bilateral Relations*, edited by Simon Shen and Shaun Breslin. London: Lexington Books, pp. 13–44.

Weiss, J. C. 2014. *Powerful Patriots: Nationalist Protest in China's Foreign Relations*. New York, NY: Oxford University Press.

Woods, Jackson and Bruce Dickson. 2017. Victims and Patriots: Disaggregating Nationalism in Urban China. *Journal of Contemporary China*, 26(104), 167–182.

Wu, X. 2007. *Chinese Cyber Nationalism: Evolution, Characteristics, and Implications*. Lanham, ML: Lexington Books.

Xu, Ben. 2001. Chinese Populist Nationalism: Its Intellectual Politics and Moral Dilemma. *Representations*, 76(1), 120–140.

Zhang, Marina Yue and Bruce W. Stening. 2010. *China 2.0: The Transformation of an Emerging Superpower? And the New Opportunities*. Upper Saddle River, NJ: John Wiley & Sons.

Zhao, Suisheng. 1998. A State-Led Nationalism: The Patriotic Education Campaign in Post-Tiananmen China. *Communist and Post-Communist Studies*, 31(3), 287–302.

Zhao, Suisheng. 2004. *A Nation-State by Construction: Dynamics of Modern Chinese Nationalism*. Redwood City, CA: Stanford University Press.

Zhao, Suisheng. 2005. China's Pragmatic Nationalism: Is It Manageable? *The Washington Quarterly*, 29(1), 131–144.

Zheng, Y. 1999. *Discovering Chinese Nationalism in China: Modernization, Identity, and International Relations*. Cambridge, UK: Cambridge University Press.

6 Conclusions and new challenges

This study presents a cyberdualistic picture of the educated young elite. Internet exposure to horizontal communication among netizens and to vertical communication between government and netizens yield different results. Statistical evidence confirms that exposure to horizontal communication promotes democratic orientation, enhances political resistance to indoctrination, and boosts popular nationalism. By contrast, exposure to vertical communication increases regime support and, at a less significant level, decreases democratic orientation and elevates official patriotism.

The Chinese government also manages to promote regime support, reduce resistance to political education, and enhance official patriotism via the Internet indirectly. People who perceive the Internet as a tool helping government officials understand public opinion and the blogs or microblogs of officials as a means of facilitating the establishment of an open government tend to attend political education courses, support the regime, and become patriots. Although cross-cutting relationships are found in the statistical analysis – that is, exposure to government websites endorses popular nationalism and the positive perception of the blogs or microblogs of officials enhances democratic orientations – the general picture is clear; on one hand, exposure to vertical communication between government and netizens tends to legitimize the regime, sustain the ruling ideology, and maintain regime support; on the other hand, exposure to horizontal communication among netizens is inclined to enhance democratic orientation, encourage resistance to political indoctrination, and fuel popular nationalism independent of the state.

To answer the "so what" question, we have to first understand the underlying mechanisms of this cyberdualism. The essential features of the Internet – great accessibility, compression of time and space, and decentralization – reinforce pluralism that is manifested in the exposure to diverse horizontal communication venues in cyberspace, including blogs/microblogs, bulletin board system

(BBS) forums, web encyclopedias, and various online news sources. The more horizontal communication venues one is exposed to, the more likely one is to remain free from the fragmentation and isolation that Habermas has warned against, and the more one is inclined to ally with the pluralist norm. To date, observations do not confirm that censorship and surveillance imposed by the state are able to completely diminish cyberpluralism. The Chinese government must catch up with the new technological developments and launch government websites to contest for digital influence. This analysis shows that e-government functions both directly and indirectly, and the processes are hardly accomplished through top-down suppression and indoctrination. The Chinese government promises netizens the possibility to build a responsive government by utilizing the Internet, which leads to great regime support, national pride, and compliance.

In general, the overall effect of Internet exposure depends on the broad political atmosphere and the real intentions of the government in regulating the horizontal communication and managing the vertical communication. The best-case scenario is that the effects of exposure to horizontal and vertical communications converge. When real opportunities are granted in cyberspace to the public during political consultation, deliberation, and participation, the public not only becomes supportive of the regime and proud of the nation, but also actually has a say that contributes to a transparent and responsive government. This phenomenon is consistent with democracy. In this scenario, the overall effect of Internet exposure is to push for political liberalization. However in reality, the fragmentation of netizens is widely observed in different political systems, democratic or authoritarian, in China or in the United States (Herold and Marolt, 2011; Tong and Lei, 2013). Thus, further improvements are needed for the Internet to produce any essential political change by shaping political participation and values.

In the worst-case scenario, vertical communication in cyberspace is simply a liberal façade, netizens will gradually realize that the government has made an empty promise, and the room to promote regime support and national pride will become limited (only derived from smooth administration and efficient e-services). No evidence shows that online political indoctrination works on this group of educated youth elites, and thus the political effects of Internet exposure will mainly come from horizontal communication. However, if the government tightens up the space for horizontal dialog among netizens, the liberalizing effect of the Internet will become greatly restricted.

What is currently happening is leaning toward the latter scenario. Fundamentally, what happens on the Internet depends on the tolerance of the Chinese government (Herold, 2011a). Based on the concept of cybersovereignty, the state claims full control over the Internet within China. The state has recently carried out multiple political campaigns against liberal discourse on the Internet, culminating in the passing of two new security laws (i.e., the National Security Law and Cybersecurity Law). Article 25 of the National Security Law passed in July 2015 is specifically about the control over the Internet regarding the concept of cybersovereignty. The Cybersecurity Law, which was passed recently in November 2016 and will be implemented in June next year, regulates the behavior of Internet companies and individual users and demarks their responsibilities. The room for Internet companies and individual netizens has been narrowed down considerably. For example, the law promulgates that network service providers, including providers of Internet access, domain registration, phone network access, information publication, and, more importantly, instant messaging services, must require users to register using their real identity information (Article 24). All network operators must preserve network logs for at least six months (Article 21), stop transmitting and delete information forbidden by law or administrative regulations, and report such discovery to relevant authorities (Article 47). Chinese citizens' personal data and other important data collected or generated inside China by infrastructure operators should be stored within China (Article 37). All these articles enable efficient surveillance and censorship, grant the state easy access to the information of individual netizens, and thereby encourage self-censorship. "(T)he law will tighten restrictions on China's internet, already subject to the world's most sophisticated online censorship mechanism" (The Guardian, November 7, 2016).

The Cybersecurity Law forces Internet service providers to side with the state and impose strong and efficient censorship that may deter netizens. Nevertheless, many modes of participation available nowadays can be deemed as "political" even if they are seemingly unrelated to politics. For those netizens who believe that they will never cross the line, this condition is mostly perceived as irrelevant (Herold, 2011b). The widespread usage of smartphones may also empower netizens in the areas tolerated by the state. According to the CNNIC data, 92.5 percent of the total Chinese Internet users use smartphones to access the Internet (CNNIC, July 2016). Smartphones intensify one's Internet exposure by granting great Internet accessibility. The wide usage of smartphones has led to the strong adoption of mobile instant messaging apps, such as WhatsApp and WeChat, over the past several years. As a result, these new apps have swiftly dominated horizontal communication in cyberspace. WeChat, which was developed by China's largest Internet company Tencent, rapidly leads the market of mobile messaging apps in this country with 700 million monthly active users, 10 million WeChat official accounts, and 700,000 WeChat articles published per day (WalkTheChat, 2016). More than half of WeChat users (55.1 percent) have more than 100 friends on WeChat as of 2015, and many of them (61 percent) open WeChat more than 10 times per day (WalkTheChat, 2016). Thus, the explosion of information complicates the management and filtering of data for companies (WalkTheChat, 2016). Meanwhile, online activism, such as whistle-blowing, citizen journalism, and cyberactivism, may be intensified.

But the downside is that WeChat users are more interested in pictures, texts, and videos than articles that are analytical (WalkTheChat, 2016). According to the Kantar data on WeChat reads, the younger generation tends to be more interested in entertainment rather than in news and public affairs than older generations. Moreover, the pool of social media users grows over time, along with an increasing number of people who tend to become uncomfortable with the duplicate and fragmented content on social media and the hyperpenetration of the Internet into their private lives. Some people have even forgone social media (Kantar China Insights, 2015). Although the final outcome of this digital fatigue remains uncertain, further technological development may weaken rather than reinforce the political effects of the Internet.

References

China Adopts a Tough Cyber-Security Law. Foreign Firms Are Worried. 12 November 2016. *The Economist*. Retrieved from www.economist.com/news/china/21710001-foreign-firms-are-worried-china-adopts-tough-cyber-security-law.

China Internet Network Information Center (CNNIC). July 2016. *The Statistical (Semiannual) Reports of Internet Development in China* (zhongguo hulianwangluo fazhan zhuangkuang tongji baogao). Retrieved from www.cnnic.cn/research/zx/qwfb/.

China's New Cybersecurity Law Sparks Fresh Censorship and Espionage Fears. 7 November 2016. *The Guardian*. Retrieved from www.theguardian.com/world/2016/nov/07/chinas-new-cybersecurity-law-sparks-fresh-censorship-and-espionage-fears.

Herold, David K. 2011a. Introduction: Noise, Spectacle, Politics: Carnival in Chinese Cyberspace. In *Online Society in China: Creating, Celebrating and Instrumentalising the Online Carnival*, edited by David Kurt Herold and Peter Marolt. New York: Routledge, pp. 1–20.

Herold, David K. 2011b. Conclusion: Netizens and Citizens, Cyberspace and Modern China. In *Online Society in China: Creating, Celebrating and Instrumentalising the Online Carnival*, edited by David Kurt Herold and Peter Marolt. New York: Routledge, pp. 200–208.

Herold, David Kurt and Peter Marolt (eds.). 2011. *Online Society in China: Creating, Celebrating and Instrumentalising the Online Carnival*. New York: Routledge.

Kantar China Insights. *Kantar China Social Media Impact Report 2015*. Retrieved from http://us.kantar.com/tech/social/2015/kantar-china-social-media-impact-report-2015/.

Tong, Yanqi and Shaohua Lei. 2013. *Social Protest in Contemporary China, 2003–2010: Transitional Pains and Regime Legitimacy*. New York: Routledge.

WalkTheChat. *WeChat Impact Report 2016*. Retrieved from https://walkthechat.com/wechat-impact-report-2016/.

Appendix
Descriptive summaries

Variables	Obs.	Mean	Std. Dev.	Min	Max
Components of Dependent Variables					
Democratic Orientations					
Ordinary people do not need to participate in political decision-making if political leaders are competent and trustworthy (5-point Likert scale).	1271	1.931	1.069	1	5
Competitive elections should be used to elect local officials (five-point Likert scale).	1270	3.939	0.967	1	5
Everyone has freedom of speech regardless of his or her attitudes or beliefs (5-point Likert scale).	1272	4.325	0.898	1	5
Regime Support					
We are obligated to support and defend the socialist political structure in our country (5-point Likert scale).	1271	4.053	1.038	1	5
I feel proud of our socialist China (5-point Likert scale).	1272	3.864	1.143	1	5
Sometimes individual rights have to give way to collective interests (5-point Likert scale).	1272	3.781	1.121	1	5
Resistance to Political Indoctrination (absence = 1)	1280	0.527	0.499	0	1
Nationalism					
I feel proud of our socialist China (5-point Likert scale).	1272	3.864	1.143	1	5

(*Continued*)

Variables	Obs.	Mean	Std. Dev.	Min	Max
I am fully confident that China will become an economic superpower in the 21st century (5-point Likert scale).	1272	3.746	1.075	1	5
Becoming the top military superpower in the world is the goal of China for the 21st century (5-point Likert scale).	1275	2.718	1.215	1	5
Online petition against a foreign country/enterprise (organizer = 2; participant = 1)	1280	0.066	0.267	0	2
Online celebration of a Chinese festival or important national event (organizer = 2; participant = 1)	1280	0.196	0.424	0	2
Independent Variables					
Exposure to government websites	1280	1.515	0.556	1	4
Exposure to horizontal communication	1280	2.295	1.266	0	4
Internet age	1232	6.963	3.189	1	24
Internet time	1240	2.893	2.194	0	18
Internet helping officials understand public opinion	1272	3.409	1.283	1	5
Officials' blogs helping build an open government	1274	3.334	1.241	1	5
Newspaper time	1280	0.353	0.497	0	7.1429
TV time	1280	0.445	0.853	0	8
Radio time	1280	0.085	0.252	0	2.8571
CCP membership	1280	0.136	0.343	0	1
Economic background	1251	778.081	467.405	0	6500
Parents' educational attainments	1265	9.128	3.356	2	16
Parents' party memberships	1280	0.509	0.691	0	2
University ID (teaching = 1)	1280	0.415	0.493	0	1
Gender (male = 1)	1280	0.420	0.494	0	1
Age	1280	20.187	1.431	16	27

Index